Detecting and Sharing Perspectives Using Causals in Japanese

Hituzi Linguistics in English

No. 1	Lexical Borrowing and its Impact on English	Makimi Kimura-Kano
No. 2	From a Subordinate Clause to an Independent Clause	Yuko Higashiizumi
No. 3	ModalP and Subjunctive Present	Tadao Nomura
No. 4	A Historical Study of Referent Honorifics in Japanese	Takashi Nagata
No. 5	Communicating Skills of Intention	Tsutomu Sakamoto
No. 6	A Pragmatic Approach to the Generation and Gender Gap in Japanese Politeness Strategies	Toshihiko Suzuki
No. 7	Japanese Women's Listening Behavior in Face-to-face Conversation	Sachie Miyazaki
No. 8	An Enterprise in the Cognitive Science of Language	Tetsuya Sano et al.
No. 9	Syntactic Structure and Silence	Hisao Tokisaki
No. 10	The Development of the Nominal Plural Forms in Early Middle English	Ryuichi Hotta
No. 11	Chunking and Instruction	Takayuki Nakamori
No. 12	Detecting and Sharing Perspectives Using Causals in Japanese	Ryoko Uno
No. 13	Discourse Representation of Temporal Relations in the So-Called Head-Internal Relatives	Kuniyoshi Ishikawa
No. 14	Features and Roles of Filled Pauses in Speech Communication	Michiko Watanabe
No. 15	Japanese Loanword Phonology	Masahiko Mutsukawa

Hituzi Linguistics in English No. 12

Detecting and Sharing Perspectives Using Causals in Japanese

Ryoko Uno

Hituzi Syobo Publishing

Copyright © Ryoko Uno 2009
First published 2009

Author: Ryoko Uno

All rights reserved. Except for the quotation of short passages for the purposes of criticism and review, no part of this publication may be reproduced, stored in a retrieval system, or transmitted in any form or by any means, electronic, mechanical, photocopying, recording or otherwise, without the written prior permission of the publisher.
In case of photocopying and electronic copying and retrieval from network personally, permission will be given on receipts of payment and making inquiries. For details please contact us through e-mail. Our e-mail address is given below.

Book Design © Hirokazu Mukai (glyph)

Hituzi Syobo Publishing
Yamato bldg. 2F, 2-1-2 Sengoku Bunkyo-ku Tokyo, Japan
112-0011

phone +81-3-5319-4916 fax +81-3-5319-4917
e-mail: toiawase@hituzi.co.jp
http://www.hituzi.co.jp/
postal transfer 00120-8-142852

ISBN978-4-89476-405-7
Printed in Japan

Acknowledgements

This book is based on my doctoral dissertation submitted to the University of Tokyo in 2006.

Firstly, I would like to express my sincere appreciation to the members of my dissertation committee – Toshio Ohori, Shigeru Sakahara, Yoshiki Nishimura, Takashi Ikegami, and Akira Honda – for their patience, advice, and encouragement.

Toshio Ohori, my advisor, guided my studies from the time I entered graduate school. I have been greatly influenced by his works, lectures, and conversations with him and he has helped me to understand the depth of linguistics.

Takashi Ikegami has been my boss since I started working as a research fellow at the University of Tokyo. From his research activities, I have learned that to achieve interdisciplinary studies researchers needs to have an interdisciplinary mind.

I would like to thank Masayoshi Hirose, Ron Langacker, Yo Matsumoto, Peter McCagg, Yuichi Mori, Keisuke Onoe, and Shungo Shinohara for their guidance in linguistics.

Furthermore, I am very grateful to everyone who has reviewed parts of this manuscript, especially Hisanori Furumaki, Yuko Higashiizumi, Yoko Kato, Hiroaki Koga, Duraid Madina, Akira Nishina, Minoru Yamaizumi, and Miyako Ryu.

My gratitude also goes to Yayoi Akamatsu, Eiji Aramaki, Dominique Chen, Mike Dowman, Tomoko Endo, Ichiro Igari, Hiroyuki Iizuka, Mai Katayama, Miyuki Kawamura, Davide Marocco, Gentaro Morimoto, Kazutoshi Sasahara, Kiyoko Takahashi, Yuta Ogai, Masashi Okamoto, Kazuko Shinohara, Yuya Sugita, Keisuke Suzuki, Kanade Yagi, and Hanae Yukimatsu for insightful discussions about related topics.

This work is partially supported by the Hakuho Japanese Language Research Fellowship Program and Grants-in-Aid for the 21st Century COE (Center of Excellence) Programs ("Research Center for Integrated Science" and "Center for Evolutionary Cognitive Sciences") from the Ministry of Education, Culture,

Sports, Science and Technology, Japan.

An enormous debt is owed to Isao Matsumoto and Takashi Moriwaki of Hituzi Syobo Publishing for their editorial support. Publication of this book is supported in part by a Grant-in-Aid for Scientific Research (Grant-in-Aid for Publication of Scientific Research Results) from the Japanese Society for the Promotion of Science (No.205046).

Finally, my deepest appreciation goes to my family. Without their help and encouragement, I would never have been able to finish this work.

Contents

Acknowledgements	i
List of Figures	iv
List of Tables	v
Abbreviations	vi
Conventions	vii

Chapter 1 Introduction — 1

1.1 Purpose and scope	1
1.2 Background	3
1.2.1 How *kara* is analyzed in Japanese linguistics	3
1.2.1.1 *Kara* and *node*	3
1.2.1.2 *Kara* and the layer approach (Form of causals)	8
1.2.2 Cognitive linguistics and causal connectives	10
1.2.2.1 Sweetser's analysis (Meaning of causals)	10
1.2.3 Remaining problems	12
1.2.3.1 How to connect the form and meaning of usages	12
1.2.3.2 Continuity of usages	13
1.3 Outline	15

Chapter 2 How perspectives link form and meaning of causals — 19

2.1 Introduction	19
2.2 Background and aims	21
2.3 Perspectives and semantics	24
2.3.1 Tense	24
2.3.1.1 Content and epistemic readings	24
2.3.1.1.1 Past main clauses	25
2.3.1.1.2 Non-past main clauses	27

	2.3.1.1.3 Summary	30
	2.3.1.2 SAC	31
	2.3.2 Epistemic modality	34
	2.3.3 Perspective structures	37
2.4	Perspectives and syntax	39
2.5	Conclusions	42

Chapter 3 Static and dynamic relations expressed with causals — 45

3.1	Introduction	45
3.2	Problems	46
3.3	Do *kara* sentences express static relations?	48
3.4	Causals that express static and dynamic relations	51
	3.4.1 Examples that lie between dynamic content and dynamic epistemic readings	51
	3.4.2 Sub-categorization of speech act readings	58
3.5	Speaker involvement and contingency detection	62
	3.5.1 Connotative relations and the speaker's involvement	62
	3.5.2 Perfect contingency and imperfect contingency	64
3.6	Conclusions	65

Chapter 4 Two types of speaker involvement concerned with causal connectives — 67

4.1	Introduction	67
4.2	Analysis of *kara* with SISs	68
	4.2.1 Background	68
	4.2.2 The first speaker involvement scale	72
	4.2.3 The second speaker involvement scale	74
	4.2.4 Categorizing sentences with two scales	77
4.3	Analysis of *kara* and *node*	79
	4.3.1 Two competing theories	79
	4.3.1.1 Mainstream analysis	79
	4.3.1.2 Analysis by Miyagawa and Nakamura (1991)	81

4.3.2 SIS-2 and *node* sentences	82
4.3.3 SIS-1 and volitional content reading	84
4.3.4 Solution with the two speaker involvement scales	85
4.3.5 Reanalyzing Nagano's (1988) data	87
4.4 Theoretical contributions to Japanese linguistics: Two levels of subjectivity	88
4.5 Conclusions	90

Chapter 5 Joint attention and grammar — 91

5.1 Introduction	91
5.2 Unsolved problems with static *kara* sentences	92
5.3 Joint attention in developmental psychology	93
5.4 Extended notion of joint attention	95
5.4.1 Sharing intentionality using language	95
5.4.2 Joint attention with and without grammar	97
5.5 Speech act theory and joint attention	98
5.6 Conclusions	100

Chapter 6 Towards grammar from the first-person point of view — 103

6.1 Analysis of *kara* sentences	103
6.2 Grammar from a first-person point of view	104
6.3 Contributions to and from other areas of cognitive science	106

Notes	109
日本語の読者のための内容紹介	117
References	139
Index	149

List of Figures

Chapter 2
Figure 2.1 Interclausal Relations Hierarchy (IRH):
from Van Valin (2004: 209) 22
Figure 2.2 Potential positions (i–iii) for the event in the dependent clause 25
Figure 2.3 Past main clause 27
Figure 2.4 Non-past main clause; SE→D(E-M) 29
Figure 2.5 Non-past main clause; D(E-M)→SE 30
Figure 2.6 Notation for PAST in Cutrer (1994) 37
Figure 2.7 Perspective structures of content and epistemic readings 38
Figure 2.8 Perspective structures of SAC-1 and SAC-2 39
Figure 2.9 Nexus types: from Van Valin and Lapolla (1997: 454) 41
Figure 2.10 How perspectives link form and meaning in *kara* sentences 43

Chapter 4
Figure 4.1 Two speaker involvement scales and usages of *kara* sentences 78
Figure 4.2 Various relationships in SIS-2 84

Chapter 5
Figure 5.1 No joint attention 96
Figure 5.2 Joint attention 96

List of Tables

Chapter 2
Table 2.1 Perspectives of dependent clauses: Tense   31
Table 2.2 Perspectives of dependent clauses: Epistemic modality   37

Chapter 3
Table 3.1 Examples of *kara* sentences that express static
           and dynamic relations   61
Table 3.2 Features of *kara* sentences that express static
           and dynamic relations   62

Chapter 4
Table 4.1 Usages of *node* with respect to SIS-1   81
Table 4.2 Subjectivity, objectivity, and *kara*   89

Chapter 6
Table 6.1 Grammatical theories from the first- and third-person points
           of view   106
Table 6.2 Related works in other fields   108

Abbreviations

ACC	accusative
ASP	aspect
COMP	complementizer
COP	copula
DAT	dative
FP	final particle
GEN	genitive
IMP	imperative (verbal form)
INST	instrument
LOC	locative
NOM	nominative
NOMI	nominalizer
PAST	past tense marker
POL	polite
QUO	quotative (particle)
TOP	topic

Conventions

For the transcription of Japanese examples, the *Kunrei* system of Romanization has been used where long vowels are expressed as double vowels. For proper names, the Hepburn system has been used.

The symbol * is used to show an anomaly in the sentence. For each Japanese example an English translation is given. The anomalies in translations are not marked with *.

Chapter 1

Introduction

1.1 Purpose and scope

This book analyzes Japanese *kara* sentences (those which contain the causal connective *kara*) within the framework of cognitive linguistics. Roughly speaking, connectives express two kinds of relations: relations between phenomena in the *outside* world, and purely logical connections that are *internal* to a speaker. Temporal relations such as cocurrency and succession are examples of the first group. Japanese connectives such as *nagara*, *tsutsu* and *toki* also belong to this group. Relations such as condition, concession, and so on belong to the second group. The Japanese connectives such as *nara* and *keredo* are good examples of these. Importantly, some causal connectives, such as the Japanese *kara*, can express *both* types of relations:

(1) *ookaze   ga   hui-ta   kara   ki   ga   taore-ta*[1]
    strong.wind NOM   blow-PAST   because tree NOM   fall.down-PAST
    'The tree fell down because a strong wind blew.'

(2) *akari   ga   tui-te-iru   kara   otonarisan wa   moo*
    lights   NOM   be.on-ASP   because   neighbor   TOP   already
    kaet-ta (daroo).
    return-PAST (must)
    My neighbor (must have) returned already because his lights are on.

While sentence (1) expresses a cause and effect relationship between the events, sentence (2) expresses a relationship between a piece of evidence and the speaker's conclusion based on it. *Kara* sentences that express different semantic relationships show different syntactic behavior.

Nagano's (1952) paper laid a foundation for the current research on *kara*, and Takubo (1987) explained the syntactic behavior of the two types of *kara* by applying Minami's model (1974, 1993). However, Sweetser's research (1990) on causal connectives in general provides a cognitive analysis that can help to explain why we have these two usages. Despite Sweetser's research, some problems remain unsolved: How are forms and meanings connected? What is the relationship between usages? What is the cognitive basis of the usages?

I will begin to answer these questions by analyzing the data and focusing on perspectives. I will then determine how grammar works in detecting and sharing perspectives. This will lead on to a discussion of subjectivity or subject involvement (Maat & Degand, 2001).

In analyzing causal connectives, Nagano uses subjectivity as a key concept, while Sweetser gives an elegant explanation of causals by treating all causal relations, including (1) and (2) above, as objective relations on different levels. This reflects the tendency in cognitive linguistics that is pointed out by Honda (2004, 2005): a tendency to describe grammar from the third person's point of view. Honda argues for the importance of restoring the first person's point of view in analyzing subjective phenomena. I contend that by using perspectives we can observe the interaction between subjective and objective phenomena in addition to the restoration of the first-person point of view. This might help us resolve the problem concerning causals, which could not be explained in the old paradigm. I intend to focus on the function of the interface (Tsuda & Ikegami, 2002) between the two phenomena.

Restoration of the first-person point of view of grammar contributes to the position that sees a strong connection between language and embodiment. Currently, scientists from various fields are interested in the origins of language that are grounded in embodiment (Ikegami, 2004; Rizzolatti & Arbib, 1998; Lakoff & Johonson, 1999). The trace of embodiment in language can be detected only by focusing on the inner state of the human being who is speaking or hearing. A sentential grammar based on a speech acts (which is called 'a theory of predication') was once intensively discussed by traditional Japanese linguists (such as Haga, 1954; Kindaichi 1953a, b; Tokieda, 1950; Watanabe, 1953). My current work asks the same question again in a new context. Cognitive linguistics allows us to ask old but unsolved questions in the context of cognitive science.

In the remainder of this chapter, I review the background of the study of *kara* in Section 1.2, then I explain the outline of the book in Section 1.3.

1.2 Background

My study's foundations are based on extensive research in Japanese linguistics and cognitive linguistics. Section 1.2.1 reviews the history of the analysis of the connective *kara*, and Section 1.2.2 explains the analysis of causal connectives in cognitive linguistics. Lastly, Section 1.2.3 points out some remaining problems and examines research that can be used to solve the problems.

Researchers in Japanese linguistics have found that *kara* can express both subjective and objective relations. They have pointed out that these two *kara* have different syntactic structures. The semantic difference between these two types of *kara* can be explained in the framework of cognitive linguistics with the notion of metaphorical mapping.

There are some problems related to the use of *kara* that are still not solved. To begin with, the relationship between the syntactic aspects of *kara* that are pointed out in Japanese linguistics, and the semantic aspects pointed out in cognitive linguistics. Second, it is not clear whether the semantic categories pointed out by Sweetser are continuous or not. The theory discussed in *Mental Spaces* helps us to solve the first problem; furthermore, the study by Maat and Degand (2001) gives us a clue to solve the second problem.

1.2.1 How *kara* is analyzed in Japanese linguistics
1.2.1.1 *Kara* and *node*
The two most frequently used causal connectives in Japanese are *kara* and *node*. Nagano (1952) points out that not much attention was formerly paid to the difference between the two causal connectives. Based on seven pieces of evidence, Nagano argues that there is a clear difference between *kara* and *node*. In the case of *kara*, the speaker subjectively connects the protasis and the apodosis as cause/reason and effect. In the case of *node*, the protasis and apodosis have a cause-effect relationship without the speaker's involvement. The seven pieces of evidence are given below as [1]-[7]. To clarify the point, I will mainly use my own examples and grammatical judgments.

[1]
A causal connective is subjective when the main clause expresses the future or when it is imperative; more specifically, it is subjective when the main clause expresses an inference, vision, intention, resolution, decision, order, request, invitation or question. The connective is used subjectively in these cases because the apodosis does not exist before the speech. That is, the speaker connects the apodosis with the protasis. *Kara* can be used with main clauses that express the future or that are imperative, but *node* cannot. See the contrast in (3).

(3) kare wa   paatii ga   suki {da kara / *na node} paatii ni   iku
    he   TOP party NOM love COP because   party LOC go
    daroo.
    must
    'He must be going to the party because he loves parties.'

[2]
In Japanese, it is possible to rewrite some causal relations expressed with complex sentences, such as (4) into (5).

(4) kare wa   paatii ga   suki {da kara / na node} paatii ni   iku.
    he   TOP party NOM love COP because.   party LOC go
    'He will go to the party because he loves parties.'

(5) kare wa   paatii ni   iku. nazenara kare wa   paatii ga   suki
    he   TOP party LOC go. nazenara he   TOP party NOM love
    {da kara / *na node} da.
    COP because   COP
    'He will go to the party. This is because he loves parties.'

The adverb *nazenara* together with a causal connective expresses a meaning equivalent to 'for' or 'because.' In (5), the first sentence expresses the theme and the second sentence expresses the interpretation. Causal relations are connected by the speaker and the connective used is subjective. *Kara* can appear in this construction while *node* cannot, as shown in (5).

Note that either *kara* or *node* can be used to connect the same cause and effect relationship when used in an ordinary complex sentence, as shown in (4).

[3]
If a causal connective can be used as a final particle, then it is subjective. This means that the cause is a highly independent condition. A highly independent condition cannot be connected with an effect without subjective judgment. *Kara* can be used as a final particle, but *node* cannot.

(6) atode iku {kara / *node}.
    later go   because
    'I'll come later.'

[4]
When a causal connective can be emphasized with adverbial particles such as *wa, koso, tote* and *toitte*, then it is subjective. *Kara,* but not *node,* can be emphasized with adverbial particles.

(7) kare ga   it-ta   {kara / *node} koso kanozyo wa   it-ta.
    he   NOM   go-PAST   because   koso she   TOP   go-PAST
    'It is because he went that she went.'

[5]
When *node* is used as a connective, in most cases the main clause expresses an objective description. The following example is from Nagano (1952).

(8) yama   ni   tikai   node   hiruma   wa   hidoku   atui   ga.
    mountain LOC   be.close   because daytime TOP   terribly   be.hot   but
    'This place is terribly hot in the daytime because it is close to the mountains.'

[6]
If a causal connective can follow auxiliaries that express the future or will, it is subjective. *Kara* can follow such auxiliaries, but *node* cannot.

(9) kare ga   iku daroo {kara / *node} watasi wa   iku.
    he   NOM   go   must   because   I   TOP   go
    'I'll go because he must be going.'

[7]
If the causal connective can follow *no-da* (nominalizer plus copula), which expresses the speaker's judgment, it is subjective. *Kara* can follow *no-da* but *node* cannot.

(10) *kare ga iku no da {kara / *node} watasi wa iku.*
    he NOM go NOMI COP because   I   TOP go
    'I'll go because he will go.'

Nagano's (1952) argument was later criticized by Tio (1988). Tio's paper pointed out some counterexamples such as:

(11) *kakekomi zyoosya wa kikenna node yame-masyoo.*
    rush   going.aboard TOP be.dangerous because stop (POL; IMP)
    'Please don't rush into the train, because it is dangerous.'

Nagano argued that sentences with an imperative main clause accompany a subjective connective (as we have seen in evidence [1]). Thus, Nagano's theory predicts that *kara* will be used rather than *node* in (11). However, in (11), *node* is used.

Nagano (1988) responded to Tio. He argued that *node* and *kara* are synonyms, so it is natural for them to display similar meanings. Therefore, it is easy to find counterexamples, such as the ones given by Tio, but this does not prove the point because what Nagano (1952) has pointed out is a tendency that characterizes two connectives. Nagano (1988) presented the results of the data he had collected over fifteen years (1970-1985) to support his observation. He asked 683 people to complete a sentence with either *kara* or *node*. Here are the two examples that most clearly show the difference between *kara* and *node*, as taken from Nagano (1988: 72).

(12) *abunai   (   ) atti e   it-te-nasai*
    be.dangerous because over.there go (IMP)
    'Go away, because this place is dangerous.'
(13) *hazimete hikooki ni not-ta ga, angai unexpectedly yurenai*
    first.time airplane LOC ride-PAST but unexpectedly shake.not

( ) *ansinsi-ta.*
because be.relieved-PAST
'I got on the plane for the first time, and was relieved because there was no turbulence.'

Among the subjects, 89.6% chose *kara* and only 0.7 % chose *node* for (12). In contrast, for (13), only 0.9% of the subjects chose *kara* and 84.8% chose *node*. This data clearly shows the difference between the two causal connectives. Nagano has pointed out that *kara* has a broader range of usage than *node*.[2]

This observation by Nagano (1952, 1988) has evolved into the classification of *kara* that we will see in Section 1.2.1.2. On the other hand, there has been little critical examination of Nagano's conclusion that *kara* is more subjective than *node* in the later stages. I assume that the definition of subjectivity was not clear at that time, causing some researchers to come to completely opposite conclusions. For example, Yamashita (1986) and Kunihiro (1992) argued that *kara* connects an objective relation while *node* connects a subjective relation. Both of them resorted to the etymological relationship between *node* and *no-da* (nominalizer plus copula), which is an element that is known to be subjective.

The following characterizations of connectives are given in their papers:

(14) Nagano
These examples all <u>describe phenomena or events that are above subjectivity</u> (a), and <u>describe the objective relations as they are</u> (b). (Characterization of *node*)
(15) Kunihiro
…it is <u>subjectively judged that they are in such a relationship</u> (a) and <u>expressed indirectly</u> (b) (Characterization of *node*)
(16) Yamashita
…it is <u>based on an objective fact</u> (a) which <u>the speaker himself judged</u> (b) (Characterization of *kara*)

I want to point out that they are all arguing about two types of subjectivity. The underlined statements (a) have to do with how the world is constructed. The second underlined statements (b) have to do with how the speaker expresses the world. As a result of this confusion, even within the field of Japanese language teaching, some say that *kara* is more subjective (Takahashi, 1993, 2005) and others say that *node* is more subjective (Makino & Tsutsui, 1986). I will come back to this point in Section 4.4.

1.2.1.2 *Kara* and the layer approach (Form of causals)

What gave an intrinsic explanation to the observation by Nagano (1952, 1988) was the application of Minami's model (1974, 1993) by Takubo (1987). What seemed to be a difference between two connectives in Nagano's paper turned out to be a subcategorization of causal connectives: there are two types of *kara*, one of which behaves like *node* as described by Nagano. In addition, this subcategorization can be explained by the structure of Japanese grammar.

Minami has analyzed the relationship between form and meaning in Japanese. He argues that there are four levels involved in the construction of a sentence. The first level describes (Level A); the second judges what is described (Level B); the third presents what is judged (Level C); and the fourth expresses what is presented (Level D). By going through these levels, one can clearly articulate vague ideas or thoughts into linguistic expressions. The interesting point is that these levels are not only semantic, but also contribute to the structure of Japanese sentences. Below is a simplified expression of Minami's model, as given in Takubo (1987: 38).

(17)
Level A = Adverb of manner / frequency + Complement + Predicate
Level B = Restrictive modifier + Nominative + A (+ Negation) + Tense
Level C = Non-restrictive modifier + Theme + B + Modal
Level D = Exclamation + C + Final particle

Using these levels, Minami was able to categorize subordinate clauses. When the clause includes only the elements in Level A, it is called a Type A clause. When the clause includes Level B elements (i.e., polarity, tense), it is a Type B clause. Finally, when it includes Level C elements (such as modality), it is a Type C clause. Connectives that are attached to subordinate clauses are categorized by Minami based on these criteria. Here is a list of Minami's categorization of connectives, from Takubo (1987: 38).

(18) Type A: *-nagara,-tsutsu* <simultaneous continuation>
 -te, duplication of adverbial form <state>

Type B: *-te*, adverbial form <succession, juxtaposition>
-*nagara*, -*noni* <adversative>
-*to*, -*ba*, -*tara*, -*nara* <condition>
-<u>*node*</u>, -*te*, adverbial form <cause, reason>
-*zu* (-*zuni*), -*naide* <negation> etc.
Type C: -<u>*kara*</u> <cause, reason>
-*ga*, -*keredo* <adversative>
-*si* <juxtaposition>

Nagano's (1952) observation is clearly captured in this categorization. That is, Minami has shown that most of the characteristics observed in comparisons between *node* and *kara* are distinctions between Type B and Type C connectives.

Takubo (1987) has modified Minami's levels (1974) and divided *kara* into two types; in some instances, *kara* behaves like a Type B connective, in others, like a Type C connective. According to Takubo, *kara* can be categorized based on how *kara* clauses modify their main clauses. This categorization can be explained by the following two examples:[3]

(19) [*kare ga   it-ta   kara   kanozyo wa   it-ta]   no*
      he   NOM go-PAST because she   TOP go-PAST NOMI
     desyoo.
     must (POL)
     'The reason that she went must be because he went.'

(20) *kare ga   it-ta   kara   [kanozyo wa   it-ta]   desyoo.*
      he   NOM go-PAST because she   TOP go-PAST must (POL)
     '(I conclude that) she must have gone, because (I know that) he went.'

The sentence in (19) is an answer to the question, 'Why did she go?' The *kara* clause modifies the Level B elements (i.e. the proposition) in the main clause, therefore this connective *kara* is categorized as Type B. On the other hand, the sentence in (20) answers the question, 'Did she go or not?' This *kara* clause does not modify the proposition but rather, modifies the Level C elements (i.e. the modal) in the main clause. This *kara* is therefore Type C.[4] See Masuoka (1997)[5] for further discussion of causal connectives in the framework of layer structures.

1.2.2 Cognitive linguistics and causal connectives

1.2.2.1 Sweetser's analysis (Meaning of causals)

Since the 1980s, researchers in cognitive linguistics have started to focus on the relationship between everyday language and metaphor (Lakoff & Johnson, 1980). Sweetser (1990) especially emphasized metaphor's role in constructing grammar. Sweetser's analysis offers a clue for answering our question: What is the cognitive foundation for the distinction between Type B *kara* and Type C *kara*?

Sweetser has pointed out that logical connectives, including causals, have the following three readings: content, epistemic, and speech act (or pragmatic). For example, in the case of causal connectives, the causal relationship between events that exist in the domain of the socio-physical relationship (content domain) is used to understand the relationships between epistemic states (epistemic domain) or the mechanism of speech acts (speech act domain). These three domains are used to explain the pragmatic ambiguity of logical connectives (e.g., *because, although, and, or, but* and *if*) and the pragmatic ambiguity of perceptual verbs and modal auxiliaries. In other words, there is a metaphorical mapping between the domains. The essence of metaphor is to understand something using the structure of some other thing that is more familiar to us (Lakoff & Johnson, 1980). Semantic extensions explained in Sweetser's book are examples of metaphoric mappings from socio-physical causation (content domain) to the relationship between premises and conclusions (epistemic domain) or the mechanisms of the speech act (speech act domain).

Let's examine Sweetser's analysis of causal connectives with examples (1990: 77):

(21) Content reading
   John came back because he loved her.
(22) Epistemic reading
   John (must have) loved her, because he came back.
(23) Speech act reading
   What are you doing tonight, because there's a good movie on.

In (21), which is an example of content reading, the speaker says that John's love caused John to come back. What is conveyed is a cause and effect relationship in the real world. In sentence (22), which gives an epistemic reading, the speaker's knowledge of John's return causes the speaker to conclude that John loved her. Sweetser roughly explains (23)'s meaning as follows, 'I ask you what you are doing tonight because I want to suggest that we go to see this good movie' (Sweetser, 1990: 77). Thus, a causal relationship is established between the enabling condition of a question and the question itself.

This categorization can be applied to Japanese sentences (Ohori, 1992), especially *kara* sentences (Higashiizumi, 2006; Uno, 2001). For example, the sentence in (24) can be understood as a relationship between events in the sociophysical world, e.g., 'A strong wind resulted in the tree falling over.'

(24) Content reading
ookaze   ga   hui-ta   kara   ki   ga   taore-ta.
strong.wind NOM   blow-PAST because tree NOM   fall.down-PAST
'The tree fell down because a strong wind blew.'

The sentence in (25) does not express a causal relationship in the socio-physical world. 'The light's being on' does not cause 'his being in the room.' Instead, the protasis shows the speaker's knowledge and the apodosis shows the speaker's conclusion. The causal relationship exists between 'I know that the lights are on' and 'I conclude that he is in his room.' The epistemic world is understood on the basis of our knowledge of how the socio-physical world is structured.

(25) Epistemic reading
akari ga   tui-te-iru   kara   otonarisan wa   moo
light   NOM   be.on-ASP   because   neighbor   TOP   already
kaet-ta   (daroo).
return-PAST   (must)
'My neighbor (must have) returned already because his lights are on.'

In (26), the speaker recognizes that the child is noisy. This recognition leads to the speaker's speech act: 'Be quiet!' Here, we can see a mapping of the causal relationship in the physical world onto the speech pattern.

(26) Speech act reading
urusai   kara   sizukani si-nasai.
be.noisy because be.quiet do (IMP)

'You should be quiet (=Please be quiet), because you are bothering me.'

This analysis is based on a view that complex sentences describe the force dynamic relationship (Talmy, 1988) between the events.

The range of speech act readings is different between Japanese and English. This problem is addressed in Section 3.4.2. We can get further information about this topic from Maruyama (1997) and Shirakawa (1995).

1.2.3 Remaining problems

Compared to the analyses in 1.2.1.2, Sweetser's (1990) analysis has stepped forward in the sense that it has made an attempt to ground the semantics in the cognitive function of human beings. Two problems remain unsolved: First, how can we connect form and meaning? Second, what is the relation between usages? In particular, is there continuity between the usages or not?

1.2.3.1 How to connect the form and meaning of usages

If we take Sweetser's (1990) position seriously, it can be predicted that not only *kara* but also *nara* (a conditional connective) has Type B and C uses. However, we cannot see as clear a Type B and Type C distinction in *nara* as in *kara*. Amihama (1990) argues that there are really two types of *nara*, but this is still debatable (See Ohori & Uno, 2001). The relation between each type's syntactic properties and semantics still needs to be explained.

While there is no specific explanation for the form/meaning linking of causal connectives, we can find attempts to link the form and the meaning of complex sentences in general. There are two approaches, a functional one and a cognitive one, and I attempt to integrate them in this book.

In the first approach, functional linguists attempted to see a general tendency in clausal linkage: When the semantic units are tightly connected, the syntactic units are also tied tightly (Givón, 1980; Silverstein, 1976). We will see this approach in detail in Section 2.2 in Chapter 2. Analysis based on Japanese complex sentences in general along these lines was conducted by Ohori (1992), and for *kara* in particular, by Higashiizumi (2006).

The second cognitive approach is proposed by Fillmore (1986, 1990) and followed by Sweetser (1996) and Sweetser and Dancygier (2005). Fillmore studied the verb forms in complex sentences that express a logical relationship.[6] His argument was that the speaker's epistemic stance toward propositions affects the forms of verbs in English complex sentences with logical connectives such as *if*, *when* and *because*. In the cases of clauses with causal connectives (such as *because*) and temporal connectives (such as *when*), the speaker's attitude is either 'Actual' or 'Assumed' (regarded to be real). In the case of the conditional *if*, three types of attitudes can be taken by the speaker: (i) 'Counter-factual' or 'Counter to Expectation' (regarded as unreal) (ii) 'Hypothetical' (unknown whether it is real or unreal) (iii) Generic. Fillmore emphasizes that the epistemic stances toward the protasis and the apodosis have to be the same in a sentence. The following are examples from Fillmore (1990: 145).

(27) Actual
Because he left the door open, the dog escaped.
(28) Hypothetical
If he left the door open, the dog escaped.
(29) Counter-factual
If he had left the door open, the dog would have escaped.

As far as conditionals are concerned, Sweetser (1996) and Sweetser and Dancygier (2005) have pointed out that in addition to the epistemic attitude toward the proposition, the structure of mental spaces (Fauconnier, 1985) is reflected by the verb form.[7,8] Cutrer (1993) proposes an analysis counter to Sweetser's. The causal sentences are not yet analyzed in this line.

1.2.3.2 Continuity of usages

Under Sweetser's (1990) analysis, since readings are connected by metaphorical mappings, a discontinuity between the usages such as content and epistemic readings is predicted. However, based on the analysis of causal connectives in English, French and Dutch, Maat and Degand (2001) and Maat and Sanders (2001) argue that there is continuity between content and the other two readings.

They point out that there are two types of connectives. Type 1 includes *de ce fait* in French, *as a result* in English and *daardoor* in Dutch. Type 2 includes *donc* in French, *so* in English and *dus* in Dutch. Apparently, while Type 1 connectives can be used in content reading, as shown in (30), they cannot be used in epistemic (31) and speech act readings (32). In contrast, Type 2 connectives can be used in epistemic and speech act readings. The following examples are from

Maat and Degand (2001: 212-214).

(30) Content reading
    (a) *Le soleil se leva. De ce fait la température grimpa.*
    (b) *The sun came up. As a result, the temperature went up.*
    (c) *De zon kwam op. Daardoor steeg de temperatuur.*

(31) Epistemic reading
    (a) *La neige fond, {donc / *de ce fait} la température est au-dessus de zéro.*
    (b) *The snow is melting, {so / *as a result} the temperature is above zero.*
    (c) *De sneeuw smelt, {dus / *daardoor} de temperatuur ligt boven nul.*

(32) Speech act reading
    (a) *Tu as été très impoli. {Donc / *de ce fait} sors immédiatement de cette pièce!*
    (b) *You have been very impolite. {So / *as a result} leave the room immediately!*
    (c) *Je bent erg onbeleefd geweest. {Dus / *daardoor} verlaat de kamer onmiddelijk!*

Maat and Degand argued that we have to see variations in content reading sentences. While the sentences in (30) express a non-volitional causal relationship, (33) expresses a volitional causal relationship. Furthermore, although both (30) and (33) are categorized as content reading sentences, Type 1 cannot be used in (33) and Type 2 can be used.

(33) Content reading (volitional)
    (a) *J'étais fatigué, {donc / *de ce fait} je suis parti.*
    (b) *I felt tired, {so / *as a result} I left.*
    (c) *Ik was moe, {dus / *daardoor} ik ging weg.*

On the other hand, in a non-volitional content reading sentence, Type 1 can be used, as we have seen in (30); however, Type 2 is not always adequate, as shown in (34). (In the original article, the symbol # was used instead of the symbol * to show that the anomalies of the sentences are not due to a syntactic constraint.)

(34) Content reading (non-volitional)
    (a) **Il y a eu beaucoup de vent, donc trois tuiles sont tombées du toit.*
    (b) **There was strong wind, so three tiles fell off the roof.*
    (c) **Er stond een harde wind, dus er zijn drie pannen van het dak gevallen.*

This observation suggests that among content reading connectives, the one with a volitional content reading is closer to the epistemic reading, and there is continuity between content and epistemic causal connectives.

1.3 Outline

I start by trying to solve the two problems mentioned in Section 1.2.3: First, how are form and meaning connected? Second, what is the relation between usages? In particular, is there continuity between the usages or not?

To solve the first problem, I will integrate the functional and the cognitive approaches in Chapter 2. In Chapter 3, I will come up with a new approach to explain cases in which these are not applicable. To deal with the second problem, in Chapter 4 I will apply and extend the analysis by Maat and Degand (2001) to analyze examples that are ambiguous between usages to argue for the discontinuity of usages.

The final aim of this book is to explore how *kara* sentences express the inner state of the speaker and events in the outer world. This is how content and epistemic readings are related.

Chapter 2 analyzes interpretations of tense markers in *kara* clauses with a declarative main clause. Tense interpretation in subordinate clauses indicates how clauses are linked (Minami, 1993; Van Valin & LaPolla, 1997). I will point out that there are three types of interpretations. Two of them fit Sweetser's (1990) categorization: the ordinary content reading and the epistemic reading causals. The other is a new category, which I call 'content reading with special access to cause' (SAC). These *kara* sentences express special mental access to the cause by the speaker or the protagonist (subject of the main clause).

For example, the following sentences (35) and (36) express the same causation between the events. However, the interpretations of the tense markers in the *kara* clauses differ. The *kara* clause in (35) contains a past tense marker *ta* that is anchored in the main clause. In (36), there is no tense marker because the tense maker in the main clause is shared between the clauses.

(35) Ordinary content
 kodomo ga   nai-ta   kara   Yoko wa omotya o   kat-ta.
 child   NOM cry-PAST because Yoko TOP toy   ACC buy-PAST
 'Yoko bought a toy for her child because her child cried.'

(36) Content reading with special access to cause (SAC)[9]
   kodomo ga   naku kara   Yoko wa   omotya o   kat-ta.
   child   NOM cry   because Yoko TOP toy   ACC buy-PAST
   'Yoko bought a toy for her child because of her child's crying.'

The difference between the sentences is the perspective structure. In (36), there is an involvement of the protagonist in reporting the sentence. Only by focusing on 'perspective structures' can we explain how the forms and meanings of *kara* sentences are linked. What I call 'perspective' is a deictic center of tense or epistemic modality. By using the term 'perspective structure,' in addition to perspectives themselves, I point to the locations and the movements of perspectives. When we exchange information using sentences, we are detecting each other's perspectives.

All *kara* sentences in Chapter 2 express some kind of causation. In the examples in Chapter 3, the tight connection between the form *kara* and the meaning causation is loosened in some sentences. Chapter 3 will start by investigating the continuity between content and epistemic readings. Maat and Degand proposed to analyze causals using the speaker's involvement in reporting the relationship. I am going to argue that there is a speaker's involvement that has to do with constructing a relationship. I will give examples that are ambiguous between content and epistemic readings. These examples report on the relationship between a notion and its feature (association), which I will call static *kara*. On the other hand, ordinary causals are based on causal laws and I will call them dynamic *kara*. Sentences (37) and (38) are examples of static and dynamic *kara* sentences, respectively. Example (37) can report on a particular instance of a connotative relation(association), such as 'Whenever it is autumn, I feel lonely'; sentence (38) reports an instance of a causal law such as 'When a strong wind blows, a tree falls down.'

(37) Static relation
   aki   da   kara   simizimisuru.
   autumn COP because feel.lonely
   'I feel lonely because it is autumn.'

(38) Dynamic relation
   ookaze   ga   hui-ta   kara   ki   ga   taore-ta.
   strong.wind NOM blow-PAST because tree NOM fall.down-PAST

'The tree fell down because a strong wind blew.'

In Chapter 4, I will integrate the two analyses in Chapter 2 and Chapter 3. Two types of speaker involvement scales will be used to describe the semantics of *kara* sentences. I will apply this analysis to explain the difference between *kara* sentences and *node* sentences. Moreover, I will explain the relationship between the two notions: speaker involvement and subjectivity.

The tools currently used in cognitive linguistics are not precise enough to analyze static causals. Chapter 5 pursues the relationship between grammar and 'joint attention' to broaden the possibilities of cognitive linguistics. Joint attention is a mechanism for sharing attention with others by pointing to the object or by using one's eyes (Baron-Cohen, Tager-Flusberg & Cohen, 1993, 2000; Gómez, Sarria & Tamarit, 1993; Tomasello, 1999, 2003). I am going argue that sentences can be used to share attention with others. I attempt to show that not only one word sentences, which have a similar function to pointing, but also static causals have characteristics of joint attention in a broad sense. Static causals are sentences which can be used to share perspectives between the speaker and the listener. I will propose how an analysis based on joint attention can reconstruct the analysis of declarative sentences.

Finally, Chapter 6 will conclude this book by discussing the importance of constructing a cognitive grammar from a first-person point of view.

Chapter 2

How perspectives link form and meaning of causals

2.1 Introduction

Based on an analysis of *kara* sentences, this chapter argues for the importance of 'perspectives' in linking the form and meaning of grammar.

Tense in *kara* clauses can be interpreted in three ways (examples (1) (2) and (3)). *Kara* sentences with different tense interpretations in the dependent clauses express different semantic relations. I will show that only by analyzing the perspective structure underlying semantic relations can the mapping between tense interpretations and semantic relations be explained. In addition, I will show that *kara* sentences with different perspective structures have different types of syntactic linkage; that is, perspective structures mediates semantic relations and syntactic structures.

In this chapter, deictic centers of tense and epistemic modalities are called 'perspectives'; 'perspective structure' refers to locations of and shifts in perspective, in addition to the perspectives themselves. In the examples, predicates are underlined. 'P-D' stands for the predicates of dependent clauses, and 'P-M' stands for the predicates of main clauses.

I will analyze three types of *kara* sentences. First, there are sentences that express causation between events, as shown in (1). Second, there are sentences that express causation between epistemic states, as shown in (2).

(1) kodomo ga   *nai-ta*_{P-D} kara   Yoko wa   omotya o
     child   NOM cry-PAST because Yoko TOP   toy   ACC
     kat-ta _{P-M}.
     buy-PAST
     'Yoko bought a toy for her child because her child cried.'

(2) *ko-nakat-ta* _{P-D}   kara   tabun   Yoko wa   yakusoku o
     come.NEG.PAST   because possibly Yoko TOP   promise   ACC
     wasure-te-i-ta _{P-M}
     forget-ASP-PAST
     '(I conclude that) Yoko forgot the appointment because (I know that) she didn't show up.'

(1) expresses a cause-and-effect relationship in the real world: the crying of Yoko's child caused her to buy a toy for her child. On the other hand, (2) expresses a causal relation between the speaker's epistemic states. The speaker's knowledge of Yoko's not coming causes the speaker to conclude that she forgot that she promised to come. These readings are called 'content' and 'epistemic' readings by Sweetser (1990), as we saw in Section 1.2.2.1.

While (3) illustrates the causation between the child's crying and Yoko's buying the toy for her child, the predicate in the dependent clause is not followed with a past tense marker.[9]

(3) kodomo ga   *naku* _{P-D} kara   Yoko wa   omotya o
     child   NOM cry   because Yoko TOP   toy   ACC
     kat-ta _{P-M}.
     buy-PAST
     'Yoko bought a toy for her child because of her child's crying.'

Apparently, the described relation between the events is the same as in (1). However, (3) is different from (1) in terms of how the protagonist is involved in the relation, because it shows the movement of the mind of the protagonist (the subject of the main clause) towards the event in the dependent clause. I call a special case of content reading such as (3) 'content reading with special access to cause (SAC)'. The ordinary content reading will simply be called 'content reading or 'ordinary content reading'.'

Section 2.3 will show that the tense or epistemic modality in the dependent clause of each sentence shows different behavior with respect to the deictic center (henceforth the 'perspective'). When a sentence such as (1) has an ordinary content reading, a perspective that describes the event in the dependent clause is identified with that of the protagonist. When a sentence has an epistemic reading, as shown in (2), the dependent clause locates a perspective in the speech event and designates the speaker as the 'host' of this perspective. In the case of SAC, as shown in (3), there is no occurrence of the tense or epistemic modality in the dependent clause; this suggests a strong integration between the protagonist's perspective and the event in the dependent clause.

Section 2.4 will argue that content and epistemic readings and SAC types (semantic relations) involving *kara* correspond to specific juncture-nexus types (syntactic relations) in terms of Role and Reference Grammar (henceforth 'RRG'), namely (clausal) 'subordination', 'coordination', and 'cosubordination', respectively (Van Valin's, 2005). Using this argument, I will claim that designating a speaker's construal as a new parameter in the semantic hierarchy allows the semantics and syntax to be mapped onto each other in complex sentences, using the RRG framework.

Before moving to the analysis of how the semantics and the syntax of complex sentences are linked , I will review the analysis of complex sentences in the framework of RRG.

2.2 Background and aims

In pursuing the link between the syntax and semantics of complex sentences, I will adopt RRG as a framework. As shown in Figure 2.1, in RRG, the general tendency of the semantic and syntactic linking of complex sentences is captured with respect to the tightness of the linkage, following Silverstein (1976) and Givón (1980). The tightness of the integration of syntactic components (such as clauses) and that of semantic components (such as events) are correlated. The more strongly the components are connected, the higher they are listed in the scale.

I will attempt to pursue a more localized correspondence between semantics and syntax (Ohori, 2001), in line with the analyses in Van Valin and Wilson (1993). By analyzing the semantics of the verb 'remember,' Van Valin and Wilson argued that the syntax of complex sentences can be predicted from seman-

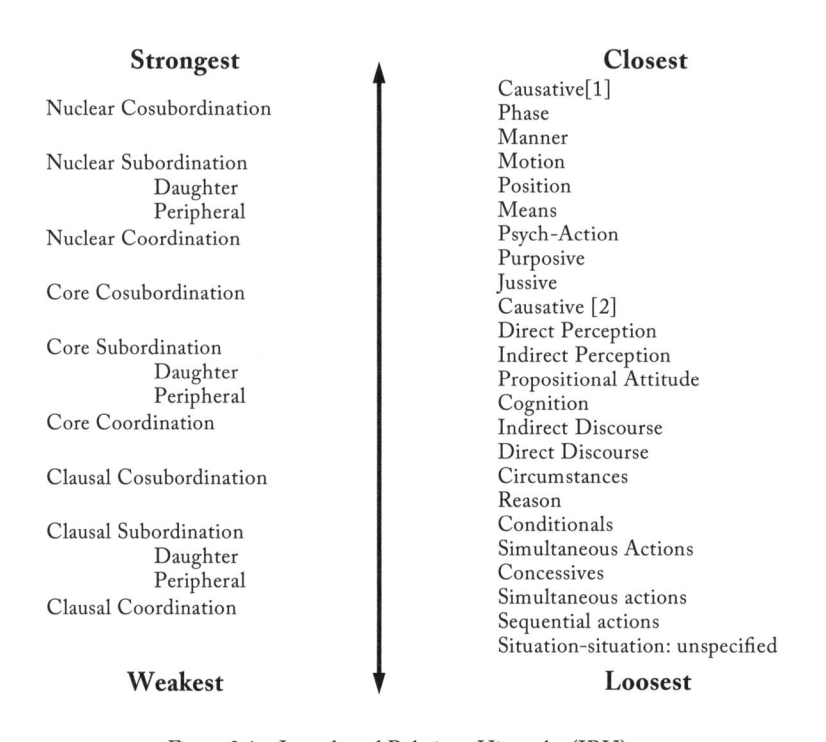

Strongest	Closest
	Causative[1]
Nuclear Cosubordination	Phase
	Manner
Nuclear Subordination	Motion
Daughter	Position
Peripheral	Means
Nuclear Coordination	Psych-Action
	Purposive
Core Cosubordination	Jussive
	Causative [2]
Core Subordination	Direct Perception
Daughter	Indirect Perception
Peripheral	Propositional Attitude
Core Coordination	Cognition
	Indirect Discourse
	Direct Discourse
Clausal Cosubordination	Circumstances
	Reason
Clausal Subordination	Conditionals
Daughter	Simultaneous Actions
Peripheral	Concessives
Clausal Coordination	Simultaneous actions
	Sequential actions
	Situation-situation: unspecified
Weakest	**Loosest**

Figure 2.1 Interclausal Relations Hierarchy (IRH): from Van Valin (2004: 209)

tics. Here, I will focus on connectives at the clausal level, and try to construct the semantics of complex sentences to predict their syntax.

The remainder of this section reviews the typology of syntactic linkage and the linking between the form and meaning of complex sentences in RRG. Syntactically, RRG categorizes complex sentences into 9 types. There are three units to be connected, called 'juncture types': nuclear, core and clause; moreover, there are three ways of connecting them, called 'nexus types': coordination, subordination, and cosubordination. Nuclear juncture is composed of a predicate; core juncture is nucleus plus arguments; and clause is core plus all of the other elements.

Functional categories such as aspect, tense and modality are regarded as 'operators' modifying different juncture types. The following list shows the operators that work in each category.

(i) Nuclear operators:
Aspect, Negation, Directionals (only those modifying orientation of action or event without reference to participant).
(ii) Core operators:
Directionals (only those expressing the orientation or motion of one participant with reference to another participant or to the speaker), Event quantification, Root Modality, Internal Negation.
(iii) Clausal operators:
Epistemic modality, Tense, External negation, Evidentials, Illocutionary force.

The difference between coordination and subordination is indicated by the structural positions of the junctures. In the case of coordination, both junctures are independent of each other. In the case of subordination, one juncture is structurally dependent on the other. RRG proposes an additional linkage type, called 'cosubordination.' The following is an example of clausal cosubordination from Van Valin (2001), originally from Olson (1981).

(4) *The delivery man having left the package on the porch, Mary opened the door and picked it up.*

The first clause is not embedded in the main clause, because it is not an argument of the main clause, and because the comma between the two clauses is rephrased with the coordinate conjunction *and*. On the other hand, the tense and the illocutionary force of the dependent clause are shared with those of the main clause. In cosubordination, two clauses share the unique operator without structural embedding. Example (4) shows clausal cosubordination.

The tightness of the integration is measured in the nexus-juncture categorization. First, when the linked units are smaller, the linkage is tighter. A nucleus contains only predicates, while a core contains the whole proposition and a clause contains even more. Thus, a nuclear juncture is the tightest syntactic relation, whereas a clause juncture is the loosest. Among the three types of linkages, coordination is the loosest.[10]

Turning to the semantic relation, the ordering based on tightness between the events seems to be intuitive. However, compared with syntactic hierarchy, the reason why we have these semantic relations in Interclausal Relations Hierarchy (henceforth 'IRH') in particular and not others is unclear. There has been an attempt to overcome this problem. Based on Ohori's (2001) proposal, Van Valin (2004) characterizes semantic relations using a decompositional system, which resembles the lexical decompositional system used to explain verbal semantics (See Dowty, 1979). Still, the current IRH lists only objectively determined relations. The aim of this chapter is to show that clausal-level linkages correlate with the perspective structures of the speaker and the protagonist.

Among the four clausal operators given above, evidentials and illocutionary-forces are sentential rather than clausal. Thus, the operators that are countable as purely clausal are tense and epistemic modalities. Both of these require perspectives (deictic centers). Moreover, they both indicate the epistemic status of the propositions contained in the clause in which they appear (e.g., Langacker, 1991). The epistemic status of a proposition concerns whether and to what extent the reported events belong to either reality or irreality; that is, tense and epistemic modals express a deictic center and how the events are organized epistemically by that deictic center.[11] This observation is the basis of my hypothesis that, at the clause level, the difference of nexus corresponds to differences in perspective organization. The analysis in the following two sections elaborates on this hypothesis.

2.3 Perspectives and semantics

I will start by comparing content and epistemic readings (Sweetser, 1990) of *kara* sentences in Section 2.3.1.1. Then I will examine SAC, and in Section 2.3.1.2 the location of the perspective (i.e., the deictic center) of the tense marker in the dependent clause. Section 2.3.2 will analyze the deictic center of the epistemic modality. Section 2.3.3 will ground my observation in a theoretical context. This chapter deals only with dynamic predicates and leaves static predicates as problems to be solved in future studies. In addition, as examples of content reading sentences, I use sentences that express the motivation and act of the protagonist (volitional causals). This is because volitional causals are free from temporal order between the events.

2.3.1 Tense

2.3.1.1 Content and epistemic readings

In Japanese, past tense is marked by a grammatical form *-ta*, which attaches to an inflected (adverbial) form of a predicate. When an auxiliary is not attached to the predicate, the verb takes the conclusive form, which expresses the non-past tense. To discuss the Japanese tense-aspect system as a whole is beyond the scope of this work; therefore, although the grammatical form *-ta* and the conclusive form are polysemous, other readings will be disregarded and I will focus on their use as past or non-past tense markers.

An event described with the predicate and expressed with past tense has occurred in the 'past'; that is, it is temporally prior in terms of perspective. The occurrence of an event expressed with non-past tense is non-prior to the time in which the perspective is located (Cutrer, 1994). Perspectives of the events expressed in main clauses and in simple sentences are anchored in the speech event. However, events in dependent clauses are not necessarily anchored in the speech event.

Below, I will show that events in content reading *kara* clauses are anchored in the main clause, while epistemic reading *kara* clauses are anchored in the speech event. First, sentences with past main clauses will be analyzed; then I move to sentences with non-past main clauses. Japanese dependent clauses precede main clauses in canonical word order.

The results of the analysis are shown in Table 1 in 2.3.1.1.3. The details of the analysis are given below in Sections 2.3.1.1.1 and 2.3.1.1.2. If you do not wish to look at this in depth, you can skip to Section 2.3.1.2 after taking a look at the contrast between the two examples given in Note 12.[12]

2.3.1.1.1 Past main clauses

The relevant events in this analysis are the speech event (SE), the event in the main clause (E-M) and the event in the dependent clause (E-D). When the main clause is marked with past tense, the event of the main clause precedes the speech event (E-M → SE).

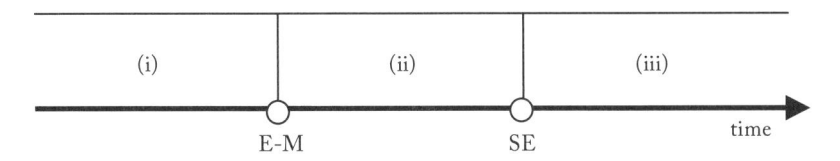

Figure 2.2 Potential positions (i-iii) for the event in the dependent clause

In Figure 2.2, the time line shows that the event in the main clause (E-M) precedes the speech event (SE). The spaces marked (i), (ii) and (iii) are possible positions for the event in the dependent clause (E-D). I will now examine what kind of sentence is used to express a case where (i) the event in the dependent clause precedes the event in the main clause, (ii) the event in the dependent clause occurs between the event in the main clause and the speech event, and (iii) the event in the dependent clause follows the speech event. Example (5) shows a content reading sentence. Contexts are given within the brackets.

(5) Content reading
[Mr. Mori's participation in the meeting is evident and presupposed The speaker explains the reason for his participation.]
Pekin   e   {iku $_{P-D}$ / *it -ta* $_{P-D}$} *kara   Mori-san   wa   tyuugokugo*
Beijing LOC {go / go-PAST}   because Mr. Mori TOP Chinese
no   kenkyuukai   ni   sankasi-ta. $_{P-M}$
GEN research.meeting LOC participate-PAST
'Mr. Mori's trip to Beijing is the reason why he participated in the Chinese linguistics meeting.'

Since the dependent clause gives the reason that the event in the main clause occurred, this is a content reading sentence. There are two choices for tense in the dependent clause, which are given in brackets. When the event in the dependent clause occurs in (i), past tense is selected for the predicate in the dependent clause (i.e., *it-ta* is chosen). When the event in the dependent clause occurs in (ii) or (iii), the predicate in the dependent clause is non-past (i.e., *iku* is chosen). This observation indicates that the perspective of the event in the dependent clause lies between (i) and (ii)—that is, the time at which the event in the main clause occurred.

In the case of an epistemic reading, we obtain different results. Sentence (6) has an epistemic reading:

(6) Epistemic reading
[The speaker assumes Mr. Mori's participation in the meeting.]
Pekin   e   {iku $_{P-D}$ / *it -ta* $_{P-D}$} *kara   Mori-san   wa   tyuugokugo*
Beijing LOC {go / go-PAST}   because Mr.Mori TOP Chinese

| no | kenkyuu-kai | ni | sankasi-ta P-M.
| GEN | research.meeting | LOC | participate-PAST

'Because of (my knowledge of) Mr. Mori's trip to Beijing (I conclude that) he participated in the Chinese linguistics meeting.'

Because this sentence expresses the relationship between epistemic states, this sentence has an epistemic reading. To express situations under context (i) and (ii), the predicate of the dependent clause must be marked with the past tense. To express situation (iii), the predicate of the dependent clause must be non-past. This observation shows that the perspective of the event in the dependent clause is at the time when the speech event occurs.

The difference between the two readings is described in Figure 2.3. The box shows the perspective of the event in the dependent clause.

| Content reading: | (i) past | (ii) non-past | (iii) non-past |
| Epistemic reading: | (i) past | (ii) past | (iii) non-past |

E-M   SE   time

Perspective (Content reading)   Perspective (Epistemic reading)

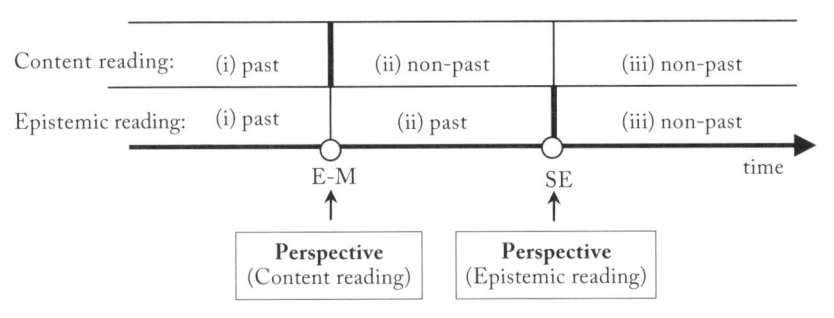

Figure 2.3 Past main clause

2.3.1.1.2 Non-past main clauses[13]

I will now examine cases in which a non-past tense is selected for the main clause. The time when the protagonist *decided to perform* the action in the main clause (D (E-M)) and the time when the protagonist *actually performed* the action in the main clause (A (E-M)) must be distinguished.

When the main clause is non-past, the speech event must precede the action in the main clause (SE → A(E-M)). However, the time when the protagonist has decided to act can precede or follow the time of speech (SE → D(E-M); D(E-M) → SE).[14] I will first examine the case in which D(E-M) follows SE (SE → D(E-M)); then I will move to the other case. Sentence (7) has a content reading:

(7) Content reading
[Mr. Mori has not decided whether to participate in the meeting or not. The speaker believes that Mr. Mori is going to participate in the meeting, and explains the reason for his participation. (Rare situation.)]
Mori-san wa Pekin e {iku P-D / *it -ta* P-D} *kara tyuugokugo*
Mr. Mori TOP Beijing LOC {go / go-PAST} because Chinese
no kenkyuukai ni sanka-suru P-M.
GEN research.meeting LOC participate
'Mr. Mori's trip to Beijing is the reason for his participation in the Chinese linguistics meeting.'

Now there are four possible places for the event in the dependent clause (see Figure 2.4). When the event in the dependent clause occurs in (i) (before the speech event), past tense is selected for the predicate in the dependent clause. When the event in the dependent clause occurs in (ii) (after the speech event, before the decision of the action in the main clause) either past or non-past may be selected. When the event in the dependent clause occurs in (iii) (after the decision but before the action in the main clause), non-past is selected. When the event in the dependent clause occurs in (iv), the predicate in the predicate in the dependent clause is non-past. The result indicates that the perspective of the event in the dependent clause lies either in SE or D (E-M).

Sentence (8) has an epistemic reading.

(8) Epistemic reading
[Mr. Mori has not decided whether to participate in the meeting or not. The speaker assumes Mr. Mori's participation.]
Pekin e {iku P-D / *it–ta* P-D} *kara Mori-san wa tyuugokugo*
Beijing LOC {go / go-PAST} because Mr. Mori TOP Chinese
no kenkyuukai ni sannkasuru P-M.
GEN research.meeting LOC participate
'Because of (my knowledge of) Mr. Mori's trip to Beijing, (I conclude that) he will participate in the Chinese linguistics meeting.'

Again, there are four places in which the event in the dependent clause may occur. When the event in the dependent clause occurs in (i) (before the speech event), past tense is selected for the predicate in the dependent clause. In all the other cases, non-past tense is selected. The perspective of the event in the dependent clause is in the speech event.

Figure 2.4 shows the difference between the two readings.

```
Content reading:     (i) past  | (ii) past/non-past | (iii) non-past | (iv) non-past
Epistemic reading:   (i) past  | (ii) non-past      | (iii) non-past | (iv) non-past
                              SE              D(E-M)           A(E-M)            time
```

Perspective (Epistemic reading)

Perspective (Content reading)

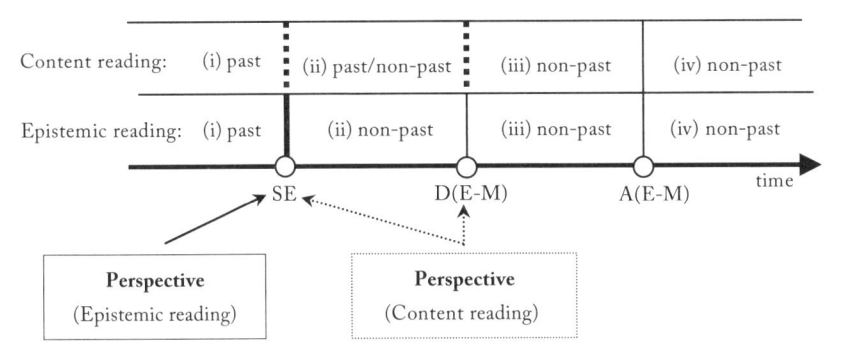

Figure 2.4 Non-past main clause; SE→D(E-M)

Now I will examine how the interpretation of tense differs when the decision of the subject of the main clause precedes the speech event (D(E-M) ffi SE). Sentence (9) has a content reading. It has the same wording as (7), but the context is different.

(9) Content reading
[Mr. Mori has decided whether to participate in the meeting or not. The speaker believes that Mr. Mori is going to participate in the meeting, and explains the reason for his participation. (Rare situation.)]
Mori-san wa Pekin e {iku P-D */ it-ta* P-D*} kara tyuugokugo*
Mr. Mori TOP Beijing LOC {go / go-PAST} because Chinese
no kenkyuukai ni sannkasuru P-M.
GEN research.meeting LOC participate
'Mr. Mori's trip to Beijing is the reason for his participation in the Chinese linguistics meeting.'

When the event in the dependent clause occurs in (i), past tense is selected for the predicate in the dependent clause. The difficulty arises when the event in the dependent clause occurs in (ii). It seems that both tenses seem to be inappropriate for expressing this situation. The reason appears to be the conceptual complexity of this situation. When the event in the dependent clause is located in

(iii) or (iv), non-past tense is selected.

Example (10) shows an epistemic reading sentence.

(10) Epistemic reading
[Mr. Mori has decided whether to participate in the meeting or not. The speaker assumes Mr. Mori's participation.]

Pekin   e   {*iku* P-D / *it-ta* P-D}   kara   Mori-san   wa   tyuugokugo
Beijing LOC   {go / go-PAST}   because   Mr. Mori   TOP   Chinese
no   kenkyuukai   ni   sannkasuru P-M.
GEN   research.meeting LOC   participate

'Because of (my knowledge of) Mr. Mori's trip to Beijing, (I conclude that) he will participate in the Chinese linguistics meeting.'

When the event in the dependent clause occurs in (i) or (ii), past tense is selected for the predicate in the dependent clause. When the event in the dependent clause occurs in (iii) or (iv), non-past tense is selected for the predicate in the dependent clause. The perspective of the event in the dependent clause is in the speech event.

The difference between the two readings is described in Figure 2.5.

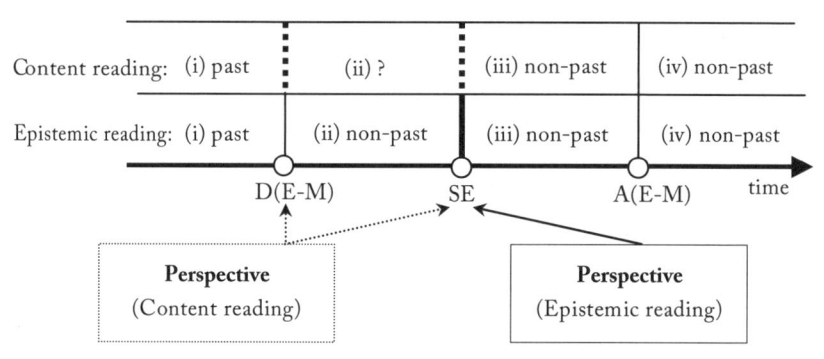

Figure 2.5   Non-past main clause; D(E-M)→SE

2.3.1.1.3 Summary

The observations in 2.3.1.1.1 and 2.3.1.1.2 are summarized in the following table. In the case of an epistemic reading, the perspective of the dependent clause is always in the speech event. In the case of a content reading, when past tense is selected for the main clause, the perspective of the dependent clause is in the main clause event. When non-past tense is selected for the main clause, the deictic center of the dependent clause is in either the speech event or the main clause.[15] The general tendency is for the perspective of the dependent clause to be in the main clause in the case of a content reading, and in the speech event in the case of an epistemic reading.

Table 2.1   Perspectives of dependent clauses: Tense

	Content reading	Epistemic reading
Past main clause	Main clause	Speech event
Non-past main clause; SE→D(E-M)	Main clause or speech event	Speech event
Non-past main clause; D(E-M)→SE	Main clause or speech event	Speech event

2.3.1.2 SAC

Some causal sentences in Japanese have dependent clauses with their tense suspended:

(11) *kodomo ga   naku* P-D *kara   Yoko wa   omotya o   kat-ta* P-M.
      child   NOM cry   because Yoko TOP toy   ACC buy-PAST
      'Yoko bought a toy for her child because of her child's crying .'

While the event in the dependent clause starts before the event in the main clause (E-D → E-M), the dependent verb is not marked with a past tense marker. The relationship expressed is a causation between the events, which is a characteristic of content reading sentences.

(11) can be compared with an ordinary content reading in (12).

(12) Ordinary content reading
     kodomo ga   nai-ta P-D *kara   Yoko wa   omotya o*
      child   NOM cry-PAST   because Yoko TOP toy   ACC
     kat-ta P-M.
      buy-PAST
      'Yoko bought a toy for her child because her child cried.'

The physical relationship expressed in (11) and (12) is the same. However, based on Iwasaki's observation, in addition to the description of this relationship, I claim that sentences with tense-suspended *kara* clauses express additional meaning. Iwasaki observed that sentences with tense-suspended *kara* clauses meet two conditions. The first is that the subject of the two clauses must be different. Compare (13) and (14).

(13) *sensei   ga   okoru* P-D *kara   gakusei   wa   sizukani si-ta* P-M.
     teacher NOM scold   because students TOP be. quiet do-PAST
     'The students quieted down because of the teacher's scolding.'

(14) *sensei   ni   okorareru* P-D *kara   gakusei   wa   sizukani si-ta* P-M.
     teacher DAT scold-PASS   because students TOP be.quiet do-PAST
     'The students quieted down because of being scolded by the teacher.'

Both (13) and (14) can be read as ordinary content readings; that is, they have the interpretation E-M → E-D. Only (13) can have an alternative reading: a tense-suspended reading for the *kara* clause (E-D → E-M).

The second condition pointed out by Iwasaki is that the verb in a dependent clause cannot be punctual if there is no description of manner. The unnatural sentence in (15) has a punctual predicate *kaeru* 'change'.

(15) **kamigata   o   kaeru* P-D *kara   kare wa   kanozyo   ga   dare*
     hair-style ACC change   because he   TOP she   NOM who
     ka   wakara-nakat-ta P-M.
     PRT recognize-NEG-PAST
     'He couldn't recognize her because of a change in her hairstyle.'

However, when there is an adverb that means 'suddenly,' which highlights the way in which the punctual event has happened, the sentence becomes acceptable, as shown in (16); this sentence can be interpreted only as one with a tense-suspended *kara* clause (E-D → E-M).

(16) *kami gata   o   totuzen   kaeru* P-D *kara   kare wa   kanozyo ga*
     hair.style ACC suddenly change   because he   TOP she   NOM
     dare   ka   wakara-nakat-ta P-M.

who   PRT   recognize-NEG-PAST
'He couldn't recognize her because of a change in her hairstyle.'

Iwasaki proposed that tense-suspended *kara* clauses express an 'observation' of the event in the dependent clause by the protagonist. The two conditions arise from this characteristic of *kara* sentences. Because protagonists cannot observe themselves, we have the first condition; and because a punctual event cannot be observed other than in the way it actually happened, we have the second condition.

As Iwasaki points out, there are counterexamples to his own analysis. While (17) has a suspended tense in the *kara* clause, it violates both conditions: the two clauses have the same subject, and the predicate in the dependent clause is punctual.

(17) *tobidasu* P-D *kara*   *kare wa   kega   o   si-ta* P-M.
     run.out   because he   TOP injury ACC   do-PAST
     'He got injured because of dashing out into the road.'

My argument is that tense-suspended *kara* clauses express special mental access to the event in the *kara* clause by the protagonist or the speaker. Here, they are referred to as content-reading sentences with special access to the cause (SAC). Let's call the sentence SAC-1 when the mental access to the cause event is made by the protagonist, and SAC-2 when it is made by the speaker. The SAC-1 sentences require the conditions proposed by Iwasaki, but this is not the case for SAC-2.

SAC-1 type sentences such as (11), (13), and (16)—that is, sentences that satisfy Iwasaki's conditions—express the protagonists' mental access to the events in the protases. What is crucial is not the 'observation,' but the mental access behind it. Thus, the protagonist need not use his or her visual perception in this construction. In the following example, there is no observation, although this sentence behaves in the same way as (11), (13), and (16) in other respects.

(18) *Akira ga   denwa   de   urusaku   iu* P-D *kara   Naoko*
     Akira NOM   telephone INST repeatedly say   because Naoko
     wa   iku no   o   yame-ta P-M.
     TOP   go   NOMI ACC   quit-PAST

'Naoko stopped going because of Akira's repeated advice.'

In SAC-1, *how* the protagonist perceived the cause event is reported. How the protagonist perceived the cause is realized as an action of the protagonist in the main clause. This type of sentence highlights the protagonist's involvement in establishing the cause-effect relationship. In other words, the protagonist's active perception (Gibson, 1962) is expressed with this sentence. The inseparability of cause and effect characterizes the access to the cause event in SAC-1 by the protagonist.

Let's move on to SAC-2. A sentence such as (17) expresses the mental access of the speaker to the event in the protasis. Compare (17) with the following ordinary content reading sentence.

(19) Ordinary content reading

tobidasi-ta $_{P-D}$ *kara   kare wa   kega o   si-ta*$_{P-M}$.
run.out-PAST because he   TOP health ACC broke-PAST
'He got injured because he ran out.'

While the objective relationship described in both sentences is the same, they express the speaker's feelings differently. In (17), there is a hint of accusation.[16] If there is no space for a speaker to feel unexpectedness (as a negative nuance), a tense-suspended *kara* clause is impossible.

(20) *tobidasu $_{P-D}$ *kara   kare wa   tasukat-ta* $_{P-M}$.
run.out   because he   TOP survive-PAST
'He survived because of his dashing out into the road.'

Thus, in SAC-2, the special access to the cause is the speaker's mental attitude toward the cause.

2.3.2 Epistemic modality

To identify the perspective of the *kara* clause in content and epistemic readings, I will analyze two types of epistemic modalities (*yooda* and *daroo*). Epistemic modality cannot be found in *kara* clauses of SAC.

Yooda expresses an inference with evidence (Masuoka & Takubo, 1992). Sentence (21) has an ordinary content reading.

(21) Ordinary content reading
[The speaker believes that Naoko assumes that a celebrity will go to the party, and explains the reason for Naoko's participation.]
yuumeizin ga <u>kuru yooda</u> ₚ-D kara   Naoko wa   paatii ni
celebrity   NOM attend seem   because Naoko TOP   party LOC
<u>iku</u> ₚ-M.
go
'Naoko will go to the party because it seems that a celebrity will go.'

Even when the speaker knows that no celebrity will be attending the party, the speaker can use (21), which indicates that the inference expressed by *yooda* in (21) is made by the protagonist.

The sentence in (22), whose *yooda* expresses the speaker's inference, is an unnatural sentence. This shows that *yooda* cannot have the speaker as the subject of inference (except when the speaker is the protagonist) in a *kara* clause with a content reading.

(22) Ordinary content reading
[Akira tends to clean up his room when an exam is approaching. The speaker assumes that an exam is approaching, and explains the reason for Akira's cleaning his room.]
*siken ga   <u>tikai   yooda</u> ₚ-D kara   Akira wa   soozi
exam NOM   approach seem   because Akira TOP   cleaning
o   <u>hazime-ta</u> ₚ-M.
ACC start-PAST
'Akira has started to clean his room because it seems that an exam is approaching.'

If we use the same sentence as (22), but as an epistemic reading sentence as in (23), it becomes a natural sentence.

(23) Epistemic reading
[Akira tends to clean up his room when an exam is approaching. The speaker assumes that Akira is cleaning his room.]

siken	*ga*	*tikai*	*yooda* P-D	*kara*	*Akira*	*wa*	*soozi*	
exam	NOM	approach	seem	because	Akira	TOP	cleaning	
o	*hazime-ta* P-M.							
ACC	start-PAST							

'I conclude that Akira has started to clean his room, because it seems that an exam is approaching'.

In this sentence, *yooda* has the speaker as the subject of inference. In content *kara* sentences, as in the case of tense, the perspective of the dependent clause is in the main clause. In epistemic reading, the perspective of the dependent clause is in the speech event.

Among the Japanese epistemic modality markers, *daroo* is said to be the most subjective, followed by *rashii*, *yooda*, and *sooda* (Noda, 1995). *Daroo* expresses something that is certain or probable that is not directly experienced. We cannot use *daroo* in a *kara* clause with a content reading, as shown in (24), but we can use it in a *kara* clause with an epistemic reading, as shown in (25).

(24) Ordinary content reading
[The speaker knows that Naoko will go to the party and explains the reason for her participation.]
*yuumeizin ga kuru daroo P-D *kara Naoko wa paatii ni*
celebrity NOM come must because Naoko TOP party LOC
iku P-M.
go
'Naoko will go to the party because a celebrity is certain to attend.'

(25) Epistemic reading
[The speaker assumes that Naoko will go to the party.]
yuumeizin ga kuru daroo P-D *kara Naoko wa paatii ni*
celebrity NOM come must because Naoko TOP party LOC
iku P-M.
go
'I conclude that Naoko will go to the party, because I know that a celebrity is certain to attend.'

It is said that the perspective taken by *daroo* is the speaker's (Noda, 1995). My

Table 2.2 Perspectives of dependent clauses: Epistemic modality

Content reading	Epistemic reading	SAC
Protagonist	Speaker	N/A

analysis is that the use of *daroo* in the dependent clause of content causals is uncommon because the perspective of the epistemic modality in the dependent clause is the protagonist in content reading sentences. On the other hand, in an epistemic reading sentence, the perspective of the epistemic modality in the dependent clause is in the speech event, and so *daroo* can be used.

2.3.3 Perspective structures

By the term 'perspective,' I mean the deictic center of tense or epistemic modality. Within the theory of mental spaces (Fauconnier, 1985), tense and epistemic modalities are regarded as indicators of mental space structures.

Following Dinsmore (1991), Cutrer (1994) modified Reichenbach's (1947) analysis of the tense-aspect system in the context of mental spaces.[17] A 'perspective' in this paper corresponds to what is called a 'viewpoint' or a 'V-POINT' in Cutrer's framework. A viewpoint is that from which other spaces are currently being built or accessed. For example, past tense is defined as follows in Cutrer's framework. When past tense is applied to space N, the viewpoint is in N's parent space, and N's time is prior to the viewpoint. Parent space is located higher than child space and is connected with one node in the figure. A 'base space' is where the viewpoint is located at the start of a discourse. The 'focus space' is where the content is currently being added.

Non-past is defined just as for the past tense, except in two respects: (1) space N is non-prior to M; and (2) space M can be either the same or the parent of space N. Below, I consider a case in which M is the parent of N.

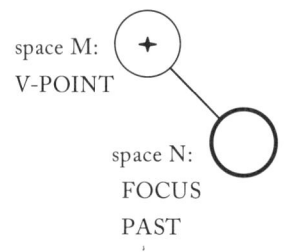

Figure 2.6 Notation for PAST in Cutrer (1994)

The contrast we have observed between content and epistemic readings can be expressed as follows see Figure 2.7. Base is where the viewpoint is located at the start of the utterance; in this case, it corresponds to the ground of speech. The speaker can directly access the events in the dependent clause and the main clause in the epistemic reading, while the speaker cannot directly access the event in the dependent clause in the content reading. The arrow expresses the mental contact of the speaker with the cause event.

(a) Content reading　　　　(b) Epistemic reading

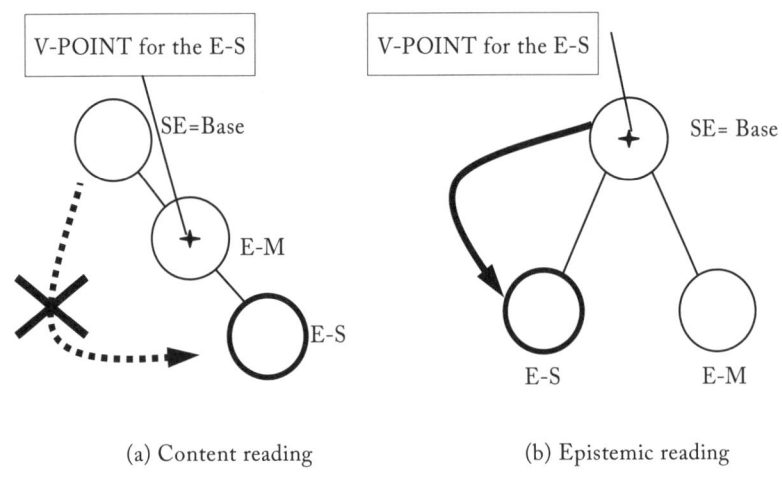

Figure 2.7　Perspective structures of content and epistemic readings

By interpreting the results in this section in the framework of mental spaces theory, we can progress in three respects. First, we can relate the phenomena that are observed through tense and epistemic modality to other phenomena that have been the subject of mental space analysis. Second, we can relate deictic phenomena to more general cognitive functions, to address the question of how humans manage with discourse and grammar. Finally, while the semantic characterization implies that the content and the epistemic readings are two discrete categories, the perspective structure given above points to the existence of perspective structures that cannot be categorized as either (a) or (b) in Figure 2.7. The perspective structures of SAC-1 and SAC-2 can be regarded as such examples. Figure 2.8 describes the perspective structure of SAC types with informal notations.

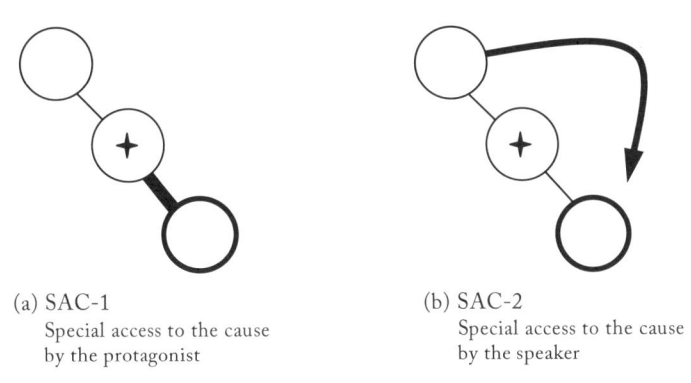

(a) SAC-1
Special access to the cause
by the protagonist

(b) SAC-2
Special access to the cause
by the speaker

Figure 2.8   Perspective structures of SAC-1 and SAC-2

Current mental space theory lacks the tools to express what we have analyzed for SAC types. However, as I argued in Section 2.3.1.2, it can be related to the problem of mental access within the perspective structure. This means that there is a possibility that by extending the framework of mental spaces, we can express the difference between SAC types and content reading causals in the long run. The topological relations between spaces are the same between content and SAC types.

In Figure 2.8 (a), bold lines show the special accesses in the SAC-1 type. I argue that the involvement of the speaker connects the cause and effect in this type. How the speaker perceived the cause is realized as an action of the protagonist. The two event spaces must be tightly integrated, compared to ordinary content reading. Figure 2.8 (b) shows that in SAC-2, the speaker can mentally access the cause event space while it is not an epistemic reading.

2.4   Perspectives and syntax

I now return to the initial problem: how the semantics and the syntax of complex sentences are linked; in particular, how the IRH in Figure 2.1 can be modified on the basis of our analysis of the data. Section 2.3 focused on the semantic interpretations of clausal operators. The three different readings of *kara* sentences showed different interpretations of tense and epistemic modality attached to the predicates in the dependent clauses. As discussed in Section 2.3.3, this distinction indicates different configurations of mental spaces, as illustrated in Figures 2.7 and 2.8.

The present section attempts to show that the three perspective structures of these causals correspond to three different syntactic types. As mentioned in Section 2.2, three ways to connect the units (i.e., nexus) are assumed in RRG. When there is no dependency between clauses, it is regarded as coordination. When there is a dependency of operators, it is cosubordination. Subordination is defined as a structural dependency.

In the RRG framework, we can obtain syntactic information as well as semantic information from operators. The behaviors of the operators show that the SAC type can be classified as cosubordination, because the operators are dependent (Section 2.3.1.2)—only one operator is shared between two clauses. The operators of the content and epistemic readings show that they are not cosubordinate. Whether coordination or subordination is at issue requires syntactic testing, as proposed in RRG (Van Valin & LaPolla, 1997). Below, we conduct two of these tests.

The first test investigates whether we can exchange the position of the dependent clause with that of the matrix clause. A matrix clause may precede the dependent clause in the case of subordinate construction, but not in the case of coordinate construction.

Sentence (26) shows an example of a content reading. We can reverse the clausal order in (26) to obtain (27), which is an acceptable sentence.

(26) Content reading
kodomo ga *nai-ta* P-D *kara* *Yoko wa omotya o*
child NOM cry-PAST because Yoko TOP toy ACC
kat-ta P-M.
buy-PAST
'Yoko bought a toy for her child because her child cried.'

(27) *Yoko wa omotya o* *kat-ta* P-D, *kodomo ga* *nai-ta* P-M
Yoko TOP toy ACC buy-PAST child NOM cry-PAST
kara.
because
'Because her child cried, Yoko bought a toy for her child.'

On the other hand, (28) is an example of an epistemic reading. When we make the matrix clause precede the dependent clause, an unnatural sentence, such as (29), arises.

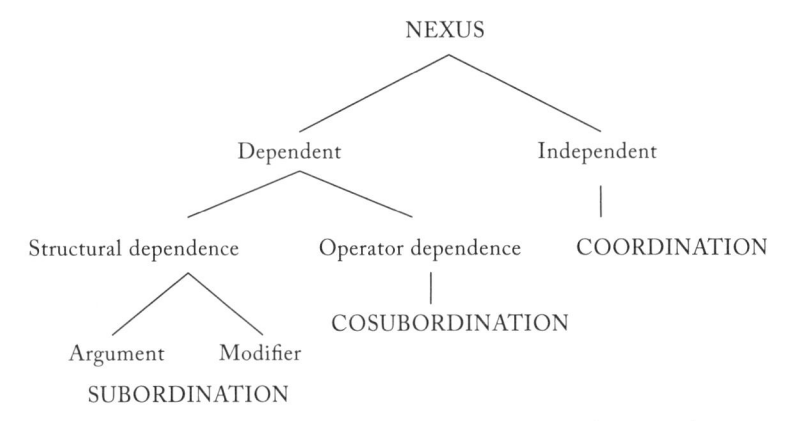

```
                           NEXUS
                          /     \
                    Dependent   Independent
                   /        \        |
         Structural        Operator  COORDINATION
         dependence        dependence
          /      \            |
    Argument   Modifier   COSUBORDINATION
    SUBORDINATION
```

Figure 2.9 Nexus types: from Van Valin and LaPolla (1997: 454)

(28) Epistemic reading
 akari ga   tui-te-iru $_{P-D}$ kara   Akira wa   heya ni   iru $_{P-M}$.
 light NOM   be.on-ASP   because Akira TOP   room LOC   be.in
 'Because Akira's lights are on, he is in his room.'
(29) *Akira wa   heya   ni   iru $_{P-D}$, akari ga   tui-teiru $_{P-M}$ kara.
 Akira TOP   room   LOC   be.in   lights NOM   be.on-ASP   because
 'Akira is in his room because his lights are on.'

Since in Japanese, the dependent clause precedes the main clause for some native speakers, both (27) and (29) sound unnatural. However, there is still a difference in the degree of unnaturalness. Sentence (29) sounds more unnatural than (27).

The second test checks the behavior of a pronoun in a dependent clause. When it is coreferential with a full NP in the following matrix clause, the nexus of the sentence is subordination. When this is not the case, the nexus is coordination.

Sentence (30) is an example of a content reading, and (31) is epistemic. The following contrast shows that a content reading allows this coreference and that an epistemic reading does not. (Two nominals with subscript 'i' refer to the same person.)

In both sentences, there is an assumption that Naoko takes good care of things that she bought by herself, compared to those given to her by others. In (30), the speaker asserts why Naoko treats the book carefully. On the other hand, in (31), the speaker asserts that Naoko is taking care of the book, based on an assumption.

(30) Content reading
kanozyo$_i$ *ga   hon o   kat-ta* $_{E-S}$ *kara   Naoko*$_i$ *wa*
she   NOM book ACC buy-PAST   because Naoko   TOP
taisetu ni sita $_{E-M}$.
be. important do-PAST
'Because she$_i$ bought the book herself, Naoko$_i$ took good care of it.'

(31) Epistemic reading
*kanozyo$_i$ *ga hon o kat-ta* $_{E-S}$ *kara, Naoko*$_i$ *wa taisetu ni si-ta* $_{E-M}$
'Because she$_i$ bought the book herself, Naoko$_i$ must have taken good care of it.'

Both tests show that the nexus type of a content reading causal is subordination and that of epistemic reading causal is coordination.

It can be concluded that, for causals, a different perspective structure corresponds to a different nexus. The analysis of the data has shown that the perspective structure is the level at which the variation of the syntactic structure can be captured. This is how the perspectives are connected with the clausal-level nexus. In traditional analysis in RRG, all causals are categorized only as 'sequential actions: non-overlapping'; by accounting for the perspective structure, we can better predict the form of the clausal-level linkage.

2.5 Conclusions

I have shown that the three *kara* constructions have different perspective structures that are each linked with a different syntactic structure. Figure 2.13 summarizes the argument.

This analysis supports my claim that perspective structure is an intermediate level to which we must refer when discussing form/meaning linking. This, in turn, supports the idea that we can create a form/meaning linking algorithm of complex sentences by using the syntactic categorization of RRG. More data are required to test the validity of my hypothesis.[18]

As a next step, I plan to apply this clausal-level analysis to other levels by breaking the categories of IRH into a set of more basic notions. Ohori (2001)

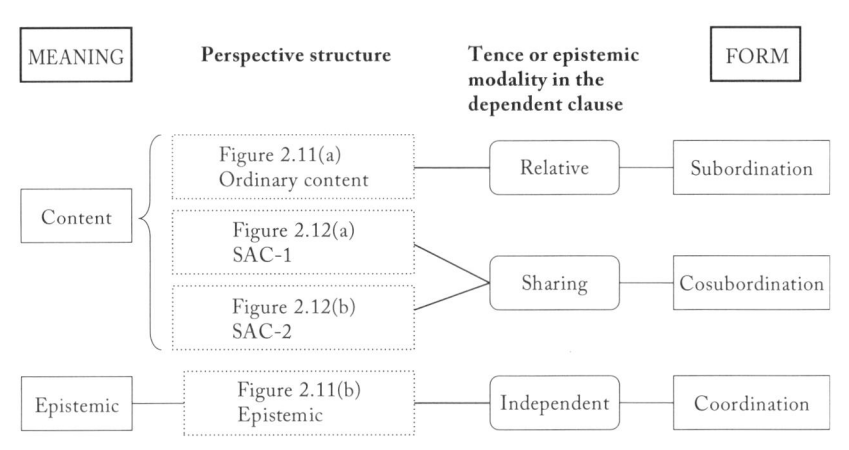

| MEANING | Perspective structure | Tence or epistemic modality in the dependent clause | FORM |

Figure 2.10   How perspectives link form and meaning in *kara* sentences

has made one such attempt. If basic notions are cognitive categories that can be testified in experiments, this will allow us to see how cognition is reflected in a grammar. Perspectives are a promising concept in this respect. For example, neurobiological studies show that the parietal-temporal-occipital junction is active both during navigation and parsing of sentences with perspective reversal, and Steels (2005) proposes that language recruits such a cognitive function for perspectives, which results in deictic expressions.

I have determined the relation between content and epistemic reading in this chapter by focusing on the behavior of deictic centers, since I assumed from previous studies that this is a promising way to connect the form and meaning of *kara* sentences.

In the next chapter, I attempt to analyze sentences that seem to have features of both content and epistemic readings by focusing on a semantic aspect that has so far not received much attention from grammatical analysis.

Chapter 3

Static and dynamic relations expressed with causals

3.1 Introduction

Causal law expresses adjacency in the real world. Expressions such as 'a leaf is a part of a tree' or 'raining causes leaves to get wet' describe relationships that belong to the world[19] rather than to our minds. In contrast, relations between concepts belong to our minds. For example, the category 'tree' has several connotations, such as 'being green' and 'making people feel relaxed.' We may say that 'green things' and 'things that make people feel relaxed' are subsumed under the category 'tree' (Sato, 1986).[20]

The ways in which language is related to this variety of relations have mainly captured the interest of researchers who study rhetorical expressions. Rhetorical expressions that are based on adjacency are referred to as 'metonymy'; those that are based on inclusion of one category by another are referred to as 'synecdoche.' Here are some examples:

(1) Metonymy
   mati ni tutioto ga hibiku.
   town LOC hammer.sound NOM echo
   'The sound of hammers echoes through the town.'

(2) Synecdoche
   siroi mono ga hut-te-iru.
   white thing NOM fall.down-ASP
   'A white thing is falling down.'

The frequency of using a hammer speeds up the construction process. Based on this causal relationship, in (1) we point to 'construction' with 'the sound of hammers.' On the other hand, in (2) being white is a feature of snow. That is, the category 'snow' subsumes the category 'white things.'[21] Based on this subsuming relation, we point to 'snow' with its 'whiteness.'

In cognitive linguistics, examples of synecdochic sentences such as (2) have been regarded as one specific type of metonymy (e.g., Lakoff & Johnson, 1987). The importance of looking at the difference between these two rhetorical expressions was emphasized by Japanese linguists such as Seto (1999) in recent studies (see also Mori, 2001; Nishimura, 2002, 2005; Sato, 1986; Seto, 1997). In this chapter, I argue that the contrast between synecdoche and metonymy is more deeply related to the semantics of *kara* sentences.

The previous chapter illustrated various types of *kara* sentences. Note that they all express a relationship based on a causal law. In this chapter, I argue that *kara* sentences that typically express causation[22] can express 'a relationship between a concept and its feature' (i.e., a connotative relation). While force dynamics (Talmy, 1988) is known to be one of the most eminent factors in causation, it is hardly evident in this type of sentence. I aim to explain how causation and association are related, in contrast to other studies, which have mainly focused on their differences.[23]

3.2 Problems

As we saw in Sections 1.2.2 and 2.1, Sweetser (1990) determined that causal connectives express a force dynamic relation in three different domains.

(3) *ookaze   ga   hui-ta   kara   ki   ga   taore-ta.*
    strong.wind NOM   blow-PAST   because tree   NOM   fall.down-PAST
    'The tree fell down because a strong wind blew.'

(4) *akari ga   tui-te-iru   kara   otonarisan   wa   moo*
    light NOM   be.on-ASP   because neighbor   TOP   already
    kaet-ta   (daroo).
    return-PAST   (must)
    'My neighbor (must have) returned already, because his lights are on.'

(5) *urusai   kara   sizukani   si-nasai.*
    be.bothering   because be.quiet   do (IMP)

'You should be quiet (=Please be quiet), because you are bothering me.'

The sentence in (3) expresses a causal relation in the real world. The sentence in (4) expresses a causal relation between two epistemic states. As a result, in (4), attaching the epistemic modality *daroo* to the predicate does not markedly change the meaning of the sentence.[24] Finally, the sentence in (5) expresses a causal relation between what enables a speech act and a speech act. Sweetser labeled the interpretations in (3), (4), and (5) 'content reading,' 'epistemic reading' and 'speech act reading,' respectively.

This categorization by Sweetser (1990) has been widely accepted and adopted in many analyses.[25] Raw data, however, contain examples that cannot be categorized easily, for example, sentence (6). (CSJ[26] indicates that the sentence is a colloquial example extracted from *The Corpus of Spontaneous Japanese*.)

(6) (CSJ)
kono miti wa magamagasii kara watasi wa toore-nai.
this path TOP be.ominous because I TOP can.follow-NEG
'I cannot follow this path because it is ominous.'

This sentence seems to share features with both content and epistemic readings, but at the same time it differs from typical examples of both readings. The relation between the protasis and the apodosis with the predicate *toore-nai* 'cannot take' can be interpreted as expressing causation between the reason for a judgment and the actual judgment; this relationship is usually expressed with epistemic reading sentences. On the other hand, this sentence behaves differently from typical epistemic reading sentences with respect to the epistemic status of the main predicate. In a typical epistemic reading sentence such as (4), the attachment of an epistemic modality to a main predicate does not markedly affect the meaning of the sentence. This is not the case in (6). Compare (6) and (7).

(7) (CSJ)
kono miti wa magamagasii kara watasi wa toore-nai
this road TOP be.ominous because I TOP can.follow-NEG
daroo.
must
'I guess I cannot follow this path because it is ominous.'

The existence of the epistemic modality changes the meaning of (6), because *toore-nai* 'cannot follow expresses not only the judgment of the speaker, but also the description of the situation. If we focus on the descriptive side of the main predicate, (6) can be interpreted as a description of a relationship between two events, just as with an ordinary content reading sentence. However, it is impossible to regard (6) as a content reading sentence, because we cannot rewrite the sentence using an explicit expression of causation without markedly changing the meaning of the sentence. See the unnaturalness of (8) as a paraphrase of (6).

(8) (CSJ)
kono miti wa magamagasii toiu zitai ga watasi wa
this path TOP be.ominous QUO situation NOM I TOP
toore-nai toiu zitai o hikiokosi-ta.
can.follow-NEG QUO situation ACC cause-PAST
'That the road is ominous is the reason for the fact that I cannot follow this path.'

Sentences that are ambiguous with respect to content and epistemic readings tend to have adjectival or nominal predicates. I assume that complex sentences with static predicates tend to de-emphasize the flow of time underlying the two events or situations. This makes the detection of force dynamics difficult.

Thus, the following hypothesis arises: There are causal sentences with *kara* that express static relations—a relation without force dynamics between the protasis and the apodosis. This type of sentence cannot be categorized according to Sweetser's (1990) framework, which is based on force dynamics.

Below, I aim to show the validity of the hypothesis, that is, to demonstrate the existence of causal sentences that express static relations in Section 3.3, and the difficulty of categorizing those sentences on the basis of force-dynamic criteria in Section 3.4. Section 3.5 explores the relationship between causal law and connotative relations. Section 3.6 concludes the argument.

3.3 Do *kara* sentences express static relations?

Both content and epistemic reading causals are based on causal laws. For example,[27] (3) contains a particular realization of a causal law (causation) such as (9), and (4) expresses an inference based on a causal law such as (10).

(9) *ookaze   ga   huku   to   ki   ga   taoreru.*
strong.wind NOM blow whenever tree NOM fall.down
'Whenever a strong wind blows, a tree falls down.'

(10) *zyuunin ga   kaeru   to   akari ga   tuku.*
resident NOM return whenever light NOM be.on
'Whenever a resident returns, his lights are on.'

As argued in Section 3.1, causal laws are based on the adjacency of the events or situations in the world. On the other hand, the relationship between concepts and their features—which I will call connotative relation in this chapter—is based on how our knowledge is structured. 'Loneliness is an aspect of autumn' and 'Cuteness is an aspect of a cat with big eyes' are examples of connotative relations. Particular instances of these relations can be expressed with *kara* sentences, as shown below.

(11) *aki   da   kara   simizimisuru*   [with exclamation]
autumn COP because feel.lonely
'I feel lonely because it is autumn.'

(12) *ano neko wa   me ga   ookii   kara   kawaii.*
that cat TOP eye NOM be.big because be.cute
'That cat is cute because it has big eyes.'

While causal law assumes a flow of time, connotative relations can be formed without any reference to time; thus, the particular instance of a connotative relation becomes a relation that is static. Because there is no standard term for the realization of a connotative relationship, we will call them the 'realization of connotative relations' or 'static relations.' The lack of a standard term and the fact that this relation is expressed in a form that relates to a different relationship may be linked.

Sentences such as (13) help us to further understand the difference between a connotative relation and a causal law. Depending on the background knowledge of the speaker or listener, this sentence can be interpreted as an instance of causal law or an instance of a connotative relation.

(13) aki   da   kara   ha   ga   irozuku.
     autumn COP   because leave NOM turn.yellow
     'The leaves are turning yellow because it is autumn.'

If the speaker or listener is familiar with the mechanism of the yellowing of the leaves, the sentence expresses a dynamic relation. Even when the speaker or listener is not sure of the exact mechanism, but assumes that there must be some reason for the yellowing, this sentence still acquires a dynamic reading. On the other hand, if the speaker or listener thinks that leaves turning yellow is part of autumn, this sentence has a static interpretation.

Sentences that behave in a similar way can be observed in natural conversation. Here are some examples. First examine the sentence in (14):

(14) (CSJ)
     moo   zyuken   toka owat-ta   kara   pattosi-tai   na.
     already examination like finish-PAST   because have.a.spree-want FP
     'Now that the exam is over, I want a spree.'

In (14), if we can assume that there must be some causal link between one's finishing an exam and having an exciting time, then (14) expresses causation. For example, since the exam is over, there is no hindrance, physically or mentally, and so the speaker can go on a spree. On the other hand, if one just associates the pleasure of finishing the exam with having a good time, then there is no force dynamic relation to be detected, and so the sentence expresses a static relationship.

Let's move to (15):

(15) (CSJ)
     [The relationship between the speaker and her boyfriend is not going well.]
     yappari   bandoman da   kara   dame   na   no   ka na.
     as.expected   musician COP because difficult COP NOMI FP FP
     'I was thinking that going out with him is difficult because he is a musician.'

In this sentence, again, if the speaker or the hearer can detect a causal chain between his being a musician and the speaker's having difficulty in getting along with him, then the sentence expresses causation. Perhaps many hindrances exist because their lifestyles are so different. However, if the speaker has a prejudice against musicians that they cannot have good relationships with their girlfriends, then the sentence expresses a static relation.

In this section, I have shown that *kara* sentences can at least express static relations that are particular examples of connotative relations. I have also shown that the knowledge of the speaker or listener determines whether a *kara* sentence is based on a connotative relation or causal law.

3.4 Causals that express static and dynamic relations

I will call *kara* sentences that express particular instances of connotative relations 'static *kara* sentences'. *Kara* sentences that express causation based on causal laws will be called 'dynamic *kara* sentences'. Section 3.4.1 shows that some *kara* sentences have the features of both content and epistemic readings, but are different from both of them. Section 3.4.2 argues that the notion of static *kara* sentences makes their categorization at the level of the speech act easy.

3.4.1 Examples that lie between dynamic content and dynamic epistemic readings

In addition to the static *kara* sentences, such as those we have seen in (11) and (12), we will address two more static *kara* sentences, each of which reports one of the following connotative relations: 'Shyness is a feature of a Japanese person' and 'Being honorable is a feature of a child who thinks about his parents.'

(16) (= (11))
    aki   da   kara   simizimisuru.   [with exclamation][28]
    autumn COP because feel.lonely
    'I feel lonely because it is autumn.'

(17) *kanozyo* *wa*   *nihonzin*   *da*   *kara*   *utikida*. [with prejudice]
    she   TOP Japanese.person COP because be.shy
    'She is shy because she is Japanese.'

(18) (= (12))
 ano neko wa me ga ookii kara kawaii.
 that cat TOP eye NOM be.big because be.cute
 'That cat is cute because it has big eyes.'

(19) *kare wa oyakookooda kara erai.*
 he TOP be.thoughtful.towards.parents because be.honorable
 'He is honorable because he thinks about his parents.'

Since the same sentence can have several readings, I restrict the reading by giving the context within the brackets. Here, we can assume that (16) is uttered by someone who is strolling down a lane with autumn leaves, and that (17) is uttered by someone who has met many Japanese people who are shy, and has encountered yet another shy Japanese girl.[29, 30] If a sentence has a dynamic content reading, it must retain the meaning when it is rewritten with an explicit causal expression between situations in the socio-physical world. For example, (3), a dynamic content reading sentence, can be rewritten as (20).

(20) *ookaze ga huku toiu zitai ga ki ga taoreru*
 strong.wind NOM blow QUO event NOM tree NOM fall.down
 toiu zitai o hikiokosi-ta.
 QUO event ACC cause-PAST
 'That a strong wind blew is the reason for the event that the tree fell down.'

When sentences (16) to (19) are rewritten with explicit causal relationships, (21) to (24) result.

(21) *aki dearu toiu zitai ga simizimisuru toiu zitai*
 autumn COP QUO situation NOM feel.lonely QUO situation
 o hikiokosi-ta.
 ACC cause-PAST
 'That it is autumn is the reason for my lonliness.'

(22) *kanozyo ga nihonzin dearu toiu zitai ga*
 she NOM Japanese.person COP QUO situation NOM
 kanozyo ga utikidearu toiu zitai o hikiokosi-ta.
 she NOM be.shy QUO situation ACC cause-PAST
 'That she is Japanese is the reason for her shyness.'

(23) *ano neko wa   me ga   ookii   toiu   zitai   ga   ano neko
that cat TOP eye NOM be.big QUO situation NOM that cat
ga   kawaii toiu   zitai   o   hikiokosi-ta.
NOM be.cute QUO situation ACC cause-PAST
'That that cat has big eyes is the reason for its cuteness.'

(24) *kare wa   oyakookoode   aru   toiu   zitai   ga
he   TOP be.thoughtful.towards.parents be   QUO situation NOM
kare ga   erai   toiu   zitai   o   hikiokosi-ta.
he   NOM be.honorable QUO situation ACC cause-PAST
'That he thinks about his parents is what makes him honorable.'

Sentences (21) and (22) are natural, but they do not express the same meanings as (16) and (17), which are used with exclamation or bias. Instead, they are paraphrases of dynamic content reading sentences that take the same form as (16) and (17), which are used in different contexts. On the other hand, (23) and (24) are unnatural sentences. It is counterintuitive to think that his being honorable is caused by his being thoughtful towards his parents, or that the cat's being cute is caused by the cat's large eyes. Therefore, (16) to (19) are not dynamic content readings.

In light of this, do these sentences have dynamic epistemic readings? The dynamic epistemic reading given in (4) can be rewritten as follows:

(25) akari ga   tui-te-iru toiu   watasi no   ninsiki   ga
light NOM be.on   QUO I   GEN epistemic.state NOM
otonarisan wa   kaet-ta   toiu   watasi no   ninsiki
neighbor TOP return-PAST QUO I   GEN epistemic.state
o   hikiokosi-ta.
ACC cause-PAST
'My epistemic state that my neighbor's lights are on is the reason for my epistemic state that he is back.'

With an explicit expression of a causal relation between epistemic states, (18) and (19) can be rewritten as (26) and (27). The expressed meaning has not changed.

(26) *ano neko wa   me ga   ookii toiu watasi no   ninsiki*
    that cat TOP eye NOM big   QUO I   GEN epistemic.state
    ga   ano neko wa kawaii toiu   watasi no   ninsiki
    NOM that cat TOP cute   QUO   I   GEN epistemic.state
    o   hikiokosi-ta.
    ACC cause-PAST
    'My epistemic state that that cat has big eyes is the reason for my epistemic state that it is cute.'

(27) *kare wa   oyakookooda   toiu watasi no*
    he   TOP be.thoughtful.towards.parents QUO I   GEN
    ninsiki   ga   kare wa   erai   toiu ninsiki
    epistemic.state NOM he   TOP be.honorable QUO epistemic.state
    o   hikiokosi-ta.
    ACC cause-PAST
    'My epistemic state that he thinks about his parents is the reason for my epistemic state that he is honorable.'

However, (18) and (19) are different from dynamic epistemic reading sentences such as (4), in which the protasis expresses the inference of the speaker; that is, the event in the main clause is grounded in irreality (Onoe, 2001). Thus, critically, the attachment of an epistemic modality *daroo* to the main predicate has no effect on the meaning of the sentence, as with (4).

On the other hand, (28) and (29) have main predicates followed by epistemic modality markers. Here, the main clauses express irreal events, and the meanings differ from those of (18) and (19).

(28) *ano neko wa   me   ga   ookii kara   kawaii no   daroo.*
    that cat TOP eye NOM big   because be.cute NOMI must
    'That cat must be cute because it has big eyes.'

(29) *kare wa   oyakookooda   kara   erai*
    he   TOP be.thoughtful.towards.parents   because be.honorable
    no   daroo.
    NOMI must
    'He must be honorable because he thinks about his parents.'

The contexts in which these sentences can be used may thus differ from those of (18) and (19). In (28) and (29), the speakers have never seen 'that cat' or 'him,' but they know that 'he thinks about his parents' and 'the cat's eyes are big' and use this information to make their inferences. For example, the speaker may know 'that cat' belongs to a species with large eyes, or have heard of 'him' from his parents that he is nice to his parents. Among the examples that express particular realizations of connotative relations, sentences such as (18) and (19), in particular, are special cases. While a connotative relationship is a relation between concepts and their features, when that feature concerns evaluation by the speaker, 'the reality for the speaker' becomes 'the speaker's act of categorization.' That is, (18) and (19) express realizations of connotative relations and categorization by the speaker.

If (16) and (17) are rewritten with explicit expressions of epistemic causation, they yield (30) and (31), which have different meanings from (16) and (17).

(30) *aki   dearu toiu   watasi no   ninsiki   ga   simizimisuru*
     fall   COP   QUO   I   GEN   epistemic.state   NOM   feel.lonely
     toiu   watasi no   ninsiki   o   hikiokosi-ta.
     QUO   I   GEN   epistemic.state   ACC   cause-PAST
     'My epistemic state that it is autumn is the reason for my epistemic state that I feel lonely.'

(31) *kanozyo wa   nihonzin   dearu toiu   watasi no*
     she   TOP   Japanese.person   COP   QUO   I   GEN
     ninsiki   ga   kanozyo wa   utikide   aru   toiu   watasi
     epistemic.state   NOM   she   TOP   be.shy   be   QUO   I
     no   ninsiki   o   hikiokosi-ta.
     GEN   epistemic.state   ACC   cause-PAST
     'My epistemic state that she is Japanese is the reason for my epistemic state that she is shy.'

Up to this point, I have argued that there are examples that are ambiguous with respect to content and epistemic readings, such as (16) to (19), and that these examples can be categorized into two types: (16) and (17) belong to the first type, and (18) and (19) to the second. All four examples express particular realizations of connotative relations, but in (18) and (19) the features include the speaker's expression of epistemic relations, i.e., categorization. This phenomenon is consistent with my observation that (18) and (19) behave more like epistemic reading sentences than (16) and (17) in these cases.

There are two more relevant characteristics of static *kara* sentences. First, as I noted in Section 3.2, static *kara* sentences tend to take static predicates, such as adjective and noun predicates. However, even when there is a predicate of this type, a sentence is not necessarily a static *kara* sentence. The following sentences in (32) and (33) are dynamic *kara* sentences, but share one of the clauses with the static *kara* sentence in (16). (16) and (32) have the same protasis, and (16) and (33) have the same apodosis.

(32) aki   da   kara   hadazamui.
    autumn COP because be.chilly
    'It is chilly because it is autumn.'

(33) kanasii hanasi o   kii-ta   kara   simizimisuru.
    sad   story   ACC hear-PAST because feel.lonely
    'I feel lonely because I heard a sad story.'

I assume that with static predicates, it becomes more difficult to see the flow of time between the situations or events in the two clauses, and thus the relationship tends to be read as static, although this is not necessarily the case. As I have shown in (13), the intensity of the force dynamics that the speaker or listener perceives determines the reading.

Second, each causal connective *kara* in (16) to (19) can be replaced with a connective *si*, which marks parataxis. See the following sentences.

(34) aki   da   si   simizimisuru.
    autumn COP and feel.lonely
    'It is autumn and I feel lonely.'

(35) kanozyo wa   nihonzin   da   si   utikida.
    she   TOP Japanese.person COP and be.shy
    'She is Japanese and she is shy.'

(36) kare wa   oyakokoda   shi erai.
    he   TOP be.thoughtful.towards.parents and be.honorable
    'He thinks about his parents and he is honorable.'

(37) ano neko wa   me   ga   ookii   si   kawaii.
    that cat   TOP eye NOM be.big and be.cute
    'That cat has big eyes and it is cute.'

In the case of dynamic causals, replacing *kara* with *si* markedly changes the meaning of the sentence. For example, a dynamic content reading sentence (3) and a dynamic epistemic sentence (4) are rewritten with *si* in (38) and (39), respectively. Sentences (3) and (38), and (4) and (39) express different relations.

(38) *ookaze   ga   hui-ta   si   ki   ga   taore-ta.*
 strong.wind NOM blow-PAST and tree NOM fall.down-PAST
 'A strong wind blew and the tree fell down.'
(39) *akari ga   tui-te-iru   si   otonarisan wa   heya ni   iru.*
 light NOM be.on-ASP and neighbor TOP room LOC be.in
 'My neighbor's lights are on and he is in his room.'

The effect of replacing the connectives can be observed more clearly in examples extracted from the CSJ. Sentence (40) is a candidate for categorization as a static causal, as well as (18) and (19). Sentence (40) can be rewritten with a paratactic connective *si*, as shown in (41), without markedly changing the meaning of the sentence.

(40) (CSJ)
 inu wa   nade-rareru   to   sippo o   hut.te
 dog TOP stroke-PASSIVE when tail ACC wag
 yorokon-zyai-masu   kara   mattaku   kawaii mon   desu.
 be.happy-ASP (POL) because absolutely cute   thing COP.
 'Since dogs become happy and wag their tails when they are petted, they can absolutely be said to be cute.'
(41) *inu wa   nade-rareru   to   sippo o   hut-te*
 dog TOP stroke-PASSIVE when tail ACC wave
 yorokon-zyai-masu   si   mattaku   kawaii mon   desu.
 be.happy-ASP (POL) and absolutely cute   thing COP.
 'Dogs become happy and wag their tails when they are petted, and they can absolutely be said to be cute.'

A causal connective in (42) is substituted with a connective for juxtaposition in (43). In this case, the meanings of the two sentences are markedly different.

(42) (CSJ)

kansya   no   kimoti tteyuu no   o   moti tuzuke-te-iru
gratitude GEN feeling QUO GEN ACC have keep.on-ASP
kara   ano   yoona   sugoi   ikiikisi-ta   hyoozoo   ni
because that like   very   be.vivid-PAST expression into
naru-n-zya-nai   ka   na   to   omoimasi-ta.
turn-GEN-COP-NEG not FP FP COMP think-PAST
'I thought that they are full of expression because they kept feeling gratitude.'

(43) (CSJ)

kansya   no   kimoti tteyuu no   o   moti tuzuke-te-iru   si
gratitude GEN feeling QUO NOMI ACC have keep.on-ASP and
ano   yoona   sugoi   ikiikisi-ta hyozyoo   ni   naru-n-za-nai
that like   very   vivid   expression into turn-NOMI-COP-NEG
ka   na   to   omoimasi-ta.
FP FP COMP think-PAST
'I thought that they kept feeling gratitude and they are full of expression.'

In (42), the protasis is presented as a cause of the apodosis, but this is not the case in (43).

The difference between static and dynamic readings is the way in which the units are connected. Dynamic causals are causal and sequential, while static causals are associative and parallel. On the other hand, the difference between content, epistemic and speech act readings lies in the differences between what is connected. I can apply both norms of categorization at the same time, because they describe different dimensions. Since (16) and (17) express only the realization of connotative relations, I regard them as content-level descriptions; because (18) and (19) express both the report of a connotative relation and the categorization based on that connotative relationship, I regard that they belong to the epistemic level.

3.4.2 Sub-categorization of speech act readings

The speech act reading is treated differently in Sweetser (1990) from the other two categories of reading. In dealing with content and epistemic readings, her argument is based on causation, while in explaining speech act reading, she does not always resort to causation. There are some examples, such as (5), that can be explained in terms of force dynamics; that is, the meaning of the sentence can be explained as follows: the content of the protasis caused the speech act in the apodosis. Other examples cannot be explained in this way. Sentence (44), from Sweetser (1990: 79), is an example. It is explained that, on the speech act level, the protasis 'enables' the speech act in the apodosis: by giving the context with the protasis, which says 'We are in Paris,' the speech act in the apodosis, which says 'What would you like to do?' is made possible.

(44) *Here we are in Paris, so what would you like to do on our first evening here?*

I will now examine how this definition works with the Japanese causal connective *kara*. Shirakawa (1995) has analyzed *kara* connectives that do not mark cause. I argue that his examples can be regarded as speech act readings, an argument that is based on enablement rather than causation. The examples that Shirakawa analyzed cannot function as an answer to the question *dooshite?* 'Why?', and it was found that they have two characteristics in common: First, the apodoses are imperative expressions. Second, the protases express information that enables or helps the hearer to do what is requested in the apodoses.

This characterization falls within Sweetser's explanation of speech act causals; that is, speech act causals express a relationship between what the speech act is and what enables the speech act, while the speech act is restricted to imperatives in Shirakawa's analysis.

Let's take a look at Shirakawa's data to check the adequacy of this speculation. He separated non-causal *kara* sentences into three subcategories.

In the first type, the speaker makes a promise to the hearer in the protasis so that it makes it easier for the hearer to achieve the request. Here is an example:

(45) Concession
    oyatu   o   ageru   kara   tetudat-te-tyoodai
    snack   ACC   give   because   help(POL; IMP)
    'You should help me (=Please help me), because I will give you some snacks.'

In the second type, protasis is a precondition given to the hearer in order to achieve the request made in the apodosis.

(46) Preparation
> *tyanto   mituke-te-oku kara   tutae-te-oite ne.*
> for.certain find.out-ASP because tell-ASP   FP
> 'You should tell him (=Please tell him), because I will find out for certain.'

Finally, in the third type, there is a course of action prepared in advance by the speaker. The protasis and the apodosis are used to present the plan.

(47) Arrangement
> *takusii ga   kimasu kara   not-te-kudasai.*
> taxi   NOM come   because   take (POL; IMP)
> 'You should take a taxi (=Please take a taxi), because it will definitely come.'

In (46) and (47), without subordinate clauses, the main clauses cannot be used as simple sentences; that is, the protases enable the speech acts in the apodoses. This exactly fits the definition of speech act causals, as proposed by Sweetser. In (45), the main clause can be used alone as a simple sentence, and the existence of the protasis helps the effective performance of the speech act in the apodosis. I will categorize sentences analyzed by Shirakawa as instances of the speech act reading causals proposed by Sweetser.

On the other hand, Minami (1993) noted that sentences such as (48) cannot be explained in terms of the usual causation.

(48) *iikoda   kara   sizukani si-nasai.*
> be.good.boy because be.quiet do (IMP)
> 'You should be quiet (=Please be quiet), because you are a good boy.'

This sentence also cannot be used as an answer to the question *doosite?* ('Why?'); thus, there is no mapping of causation. This type of *kara* sentence is different from those pointed out by Shirakawa. Sentence (48) is different from the second and third usages that Shirakawa points out ('preparation' and 'arrangement'), because the main clause can be used alone as a simple sentence. The usage in (48) is different from the first usage ('concession') because it does not create an obligation for the listener in the protasis. In this sentence, by uttering the protasis, the speaker is already admitting that the listener is a good boy, and, therefore, it is difficult to conclude that the speaker will use the admission of the listener's being 'good' to quiet him.

My proposal is to categorize (48) as a type of static *kara* sentence. The following two observations support this proposal. First, (48) is based on a connotative relationship, such as 'Every good child has the feature "quiet."' The speaker says, 'You are a good boy,' thus admitting that the listener is good. Then, by referring to the connotation in (48), the speaker tries to communicate that a good boy should be quiet. In addition, the speaker gives the imperative 'Please be quiet!' with the apodosis. The connotation underlying the sentence and the speech act are both by implication. Therefore, as can be predicted—as for the static causals in Section 3.4.1—even if we rewrite the causal connective *kara* in (48) with the connective for juxtaposition *si*, as shown in (49), the meaning of the sentence is not significantly different.

(49) *iikoda   si   sizukani si-nasai.*
 be.good.boy and be.quiet do (IMP)
 'You are a good boy, and you should be quiet (=please be quiet).'

Thus, sentence in (48) can be categorized as a static speech act reading. On the other hand, there are various categories of dynamic speech act reading. A sentence such as (5) is a typical dynamic reading. However, a sentence that does not display this dynamic nature, such as (44), and the sentences pointed out by Shirakawa—(45), (46), and (47)—which can be explained with respect to enablement, will be categorized as a dynamic speech act reading for the moment.

The following table summarizes the examples we have discussed.

Table 3.1 Examples of *kara* sentences that express static and dynamic relations

	Dynamic relation	*Static relation*
Content reading	(3), (32), (33), (42)	(11) = (16), (17)
Epistemic reading	(4), (7), (28), (29)	(6), (12) = (18), (19), (40)
Speech act reading	(5), (44), ((45), (46), (47))	(48)

The characterization of the two types of *kara* sentences can be summarized as follows:

Table 3.2 Features of *kara* sentences that express static and dynamic relations

	Dynamic relation	Static relation
Causality	Causal	Non-causal (associative)
Temporality	Temporal	Non-temporal (parallel)

The following section will explore how these two different relations are connected, and the consequences of their nature, by going back to the contrast between causal law and connotative relations. Since the apparent difference between these two relations is whether they express the outer world of the speaker or the inner world of the speaker, an inquiry into the difference between the two will focus especially on speaker involvement.

3.5 Speaker involvement and contingency detection

3.5.1 Connotative relations and the speaker's involvement

In Japanese, connotative relations can be expressed using the noun *mono*, as shown in (50).

(50) *kabin wa hana o ikeru mono da.*
     vase TOP flower ACC arrange thing COP
     'A vase is a thing to arrange flowers in.'

Teramura (1984) called this usage of *mono* a 'disposition defining usage.' *Mono* can be followed by a copula, such as *da*, which makes what is called a *mono-da* construction. *Mono-da* can be used as an epistemic modality in this construction, as shown in (51). Teramura pointed out that this usage of *mono* is continuous with the disposition defining usage. Fujii (2000) sees a process of grammaticalization behind these two usages. In this sentence, the *mono-da* construction expresses the propositional attitude of the speaker: 'We should not do bad things.'

(51) *warui koto wa si-nai mono da (to watasi wa*
     bad thing TOP do-NEG thing COP (COMP I   TOP
     omou).
     think)

'(I think that) we should not do bad things.'

The transition from (50) to (51) can be explained as follows. The definition of a disposition may or may not be shared generally in the society. When it is largely shared, as in (50), the sentence has a disposition defining usage. However, when it is not shared and the speaker's choice of the definition is highlighted, it can be interpreted as a propositional attitude.

The connotative relations behind the static *kara* sentences can also be expressed with a *mono-da* construction. Underlying the static content reading of (16) and (17) are connotative relations, as shown in (52) and (53).

(52) *aki   wa   simizimisuru mono da   (to   watasi wa*
     autumn TOP feel.lonely   thing COP (COMP I   TOP
     omou.)
     think)
     '(I think that) autumn is a time when people feel lonely.'

(53) *nihonzin   wa   utikina mono da   (to   watasi wa*
     Japanese.person TOP be.shy thing COP (COMP I   TOP
     omou)
     think)
     '(I think that) Japanese are shy.'

Sentences (52) and (53) not only express definitions of dispositions, but also express the speakers' propositional attitudes. This is why we can have *to watasi wa omou* ('I think that') at the end of the sentence without changing the meaning. When the static causal conveys scientific information, as in (55), the connotative relation behind the sentence does not express a propositional attitude.

(54) *mizu da   kara   zero do   de   kooru*
     water COP because zero degree LOC freeze
     'It freezes at zero degrees Celsius because it is water.'

(55) *mizu wa   zero do   de   kooru mono*
     wate TOP zero degree LOC freeze thing
     *da   (*to   watasi wa   omou.)*
     COP (COMP I   TOP   think)
     '(I think that) water is a thing that freezes at zero degrees Celsius.'

The dynamic causals that convey causation as information do not express the speaker's propositional stance. The sentence in (56) states the causal law that is behind the dynamic causal in (3).

(56) ookaze   ga   huku   to   ki   ga   taoreru
     strong.wind NOM   blow   whenever   tree NOM   fall.down
     (*to   watasi wa   omou)
     (COMP   I   TOP   think)
     '(I think that) whenever a strong wind blows, a tree falls down.'

3.5.2 Perfect contingency and imperfect contingency

My analysis is that the connotative relation expresses the propositional stance of the speaker when the contingency between a notion and its feature is imperfect.

When a connotative relation is an imperfect contingency, it not necessarily shared in the society. Then, the fact that at least the speaker bears such a contingency in mind will be highlighted. The report of a realization of imperfect contingency, such as (16) or (17), does not give reliable information about the world. Instead, it implies how the speaker conceives the world(i.e. the speaker's intentionality).

In this case, the speaker is not a referent of the *kara* sentence. The referent is the static relationship that is based on the speaker's association. When the speaker's imperfect contingency is explicitly expressed using sentences such as (52) or (53), then the speaker becomes a part of the referent.

When a speaker describes a perfectly contingent relationship (Gergely & Watson, 1999), the responsibility of the speaker in connecting the concepts will disappear. He or she is not the only person who connects the two units. Using a perfectly contingent relationship, a speaker can describe the outer world, since the relationship belongs to the world. Such expressions are informative. A causal law is based on a perfect contingency. Some connotative relations, such as (55), are perfectly contingent.

In developmental psychology, researchers who are interested in social cognition widely argue that imperfect contingency is related to humans' understanding of others. For ordinary infants, self is recognized as something that has perfect contingency, and other people are recognized as something that has imperfect contingency (Gergely & Watson, 1999). Autistic children are said to lack the module that detects imperfect contingency. Mistreated children also show a special attitude towards perfect and imperfect contingency (Koós & Gergely, 2001). A further analysis of linguistically expressed contingent relationships requires a theory of interaction. I explore how imperfect contingency works in interaction in Chapter 5.

3.6 Conclusions

Typical causals express causation, which is a relationship based on causal laws. By analyzing *kara* sentences, I have shown that some causals express static relations, which are based on connotative relations. On the surface, causation and a realization of connotative relations are incompatible. However, I have argued that they are complementary. The same sentence can be interpreted as either a static or dynamic causal, depending on the knowledge of the interpreter. My future research will include an investigation of the relationship between forms for causation and connotation in languages other than Japanese.[31]

Maat and Degand (2001) argued that in Sweetser's categorization of causals that express the dynamic relationship, as we proceed from content to epistemic and speech act readings, the involvement of the speaker in the expressed relation increases. This chapter has shown that in categorizing *kara* sentences, we need to think of a completely different involvement for the speaker. When we say that the involvement of the speaker is higher in some static causals, this is connected with the construction of the relationship or the display of intentionality of the speaker. I will elaborate this point in the next chapter.

Chapter 4

Two types of speaker involvement concerned with causal connectives

4.1 Introduction

This book began by posing the question: How do sentences that contain causal connectives form a bridge between a description of the outer world and an expression of the inner mind? In the framework of cognitive linguistics, this question can be reformulated as follows: What is the relationship between the content and non-content readings of causal connectives proposed by Sweetser (1990)? I have taken two different approaches to answer the question. Firstly, Chapter 2 focused on 'perspective structure,' and extended Sweetser's (1990) analysis. Secondly, Chapter 3 considered examples of causal connectives that do not fit Sweetser's (1990) categorizations. These examples are used to express particular instances of connotative relations or associations by the speaker, while typical causals, such as those discussed in Chapter 2 are used to express causation. That is, in Chapter 2, the *kara* form is tightly connected with the meaning causation, but this connection is loosened to various degrees for most of the examples in Chapter 3. I argue that the display of intentionality is what makes these two types of causal sentences continuous.

In this chapter, I will demonstrate how these two approaches (which use perspectives structure on the one hand, and display of intentionality on the other) are related, and how they can capture the semantics of *kara* sentences. Below, I will explore the concept of the 'speaker involvement scale' (SIS) proposed by Maat and Degand (2001). This is an attempt to measure the degree to which a speaker is involved in the construal of the causal relation.

In Section 4.2, I will extend the notion of 'speaker involvement.' I will show that the data analyzed in Chapter 2 of this book can be incorporated into this scale. I will then propose another scale that measures speaker involvement from a different point of view. The data observed in Chapter 3 can only be located on this second scale. The first SIS measures speaker involvement in reporting the relationship between events. The second SIS measures speaker involvement in constructing the relationship, which is reported in a sentence. In other words, one measures the subjectivity in reporting the relation and the other measures the subjectivity of the reported relation. With these two scales, we can observe how various examples of *kara* sentences are related to one another. Then, in Section 4.3, in order to show the adequacy of analyzing causal connectives with the two SISs, I will apply my analysis to the two causal connectives *kara* and *node*, demonstrating the differences between them. Section 4.4 examines the theoretical contributions of the analysis proposed in this chapter, by comparing the speaker involvement with the traditional notion of subjectivity in Japanese linguistics. Finally, Section 4.5 presents a conclusion to the ideas discussed in this chapter.

This chapter argues that the semantics of *kara* can be explained by paying attention not only to causation, but also to the speaker. Two speaker involvement scales can be used to measure the two ways in which a speaker interacts with events.

4.2 Analysis of *kara* with SISs

4.2.1 Background

As repeatedly noted in this book, Sweetser (1990) has pointed out that logical connectives, including causals, have the following three readings: content, epistemic, and speech act. For example, in the case of causal connectives, the causal relationship between events that exist in the domain of the socio-physical relationship (content domain) is used to understand the relationship between the epistemic states (epistemic domain) or the mechanism of speech acts (speech act domain). Here are examples of each of the three readings.

(1) Content reading
    ookaze   ga   hui-ta   kara   ki   ga   taore-ta
    strong.wind NOM blow-PAST because tree NOM fall.down-PAST

'The tree fell down because a strong wind blew.'

(2) Epistemic reading
akari ga tui-te-iru kara otonarisan wa moo
light NOM be.on-ASP because neighbor TOP already
kaet-ta (daroo).
return-ASP (must)
'My neighbor (must have) returned already, because his lights are on.'

(3) Speech act reading
urusai kara sizukani si-nasai.
be.bothering because be.quiet do (IMP)
'You should be quiet (=Please be quiet), because you are bothering me.'

Within Sweetser's framework, there are three different readings because there are three different cognitive domains. Domains are discrete rather than continuous, and this implies a discontinuity between forms. Against this implication, Maat and Degand (2001) claim that there *is* continuity between content and non-content readings, based on their observation of French, English, and Dutch connectives (See Section 1.2.3 of this book for a more detailed description of their argument). They believe that there is an important difference between two types of content readings, non-volitional and volitional, and that this must be taken into account. The sentence in (1) is an example of a non-volitional content reading and the sentence in (4) is an example of a volitional content reading in Japanese.

(4) Volitional content reading
kodomo ga nai-ta kara Yoko wa omotya o
child NOM cry-PAST because Yoko TOP toy ACC
kat-ta.
buy-PAST
'Yoko bought a toy for her child because her child was crying.'

Maat and Degand show that the same connectives are used for an epistemic reading and a volitional content reading in French, English, and Dutch. Moreover, these connectives cannot be used for non-volitional content reading in French, English, or Dutch.

Based on this observation, they claim that content and epistemic readings are continuous and the difference lies in how strongly the speaker is involved in establishing a causal relation. In their words, speaker involvement is 'the degree to which the present speaker is implicitly involved in the construal of the causal relation' (Maat & Degand, 2001: 214). They subsequently proposed a speaker involvement scale, in which causal relations can be ordered in terms of increasing speaker involvement: non-volitional content reading, volitional content reading, epistemic reading, and speech act reading.

Four factors are used by Maat and Degand to measure how strongly a speaker is involved. I will review these factors in [1] to [4] below using Japanese examples.

[1]
The first factor is the degree of the subjective involvement of a conscious participant (i. e. the speaker or the protagonist). To understand a volitional causal relation, the speaker has to understand that the cause and the consequences are both in the mental domain of the protagonist. This implies that the speaker needs to participate more in interpreting the causal relation in (4) than that in (1).

[2]
The second factor is how much less isomorphic a given causal relation is with a causal relation in the real world. Let us compare the sentences in (2) and (5):

(5) Epistemic reading
otonarisan wa moo kaet-ta kara akari ga
neighbor TOP already return-PAST because light NOM
tui-te iru (daroo).
be.on-ASP (must)
'I guess neighbor's lights are on, because he is back already.'

In the real world, his coming back precedes his turning on the lights in his room. While both (2) and (5) convey the speaker's inference, the causal relation is isomorphic to the causal relation in the real word in (5) but not isomorphic in the case of (2). (2), therefore, is regarded as having a higher degree of speaker involvement than (5).

[3]
The third factor is any kind of distance (e.g., spatial, temporal) between the present speaker and the causal relation. When a given sentence expresses the decision of the speaker, it has a higher degree of speaker involvement than when the sentence expresses someone else's decision. For instance, in comparing (4) and (6), (6) has a higher speaker involvement than (4).

(6) *kodomo ga nai-ta kara watasi wa omotya o*
    child NOM cry-PAST because I TOP toy ACC
    kat-ta.
    buy-PAST
    'I bought a toy for my child because my child cried.'

When the sentence expresses the speaker's decision at the moment of speaking, it has a higher degree of involvement than when the sentence expresses the speaker's decision in the past. Thus, (7) has higher speaker involvement than (6).

(7) *kodomo ga nai-te-iru kara watasi wa omotya o*
    child NOM cry-ASP because I TOP toy ACC
    kaoo.
    buy-VOL
    'I want to buy a toy for my child because my child is crying.'

[4]
The final factor is whether a conscious participant is involved implicitly or explicitly. Following Langacker (1990), Maat and Degand claim that, when the involvement of the conscious participant is more implicit, the expression is more subjective. (9) is more subjective than (8) when (8) is used as an objective report of 'him,' and that (10) is more objective than (9). However, their argument predicts that (8) can be more subjective than (10) when (8) is used as an expression of the speaker's inference. This occurs, for example, when the following speech precedes the sentence in (8): 'He can only be Japanese or Korean and I am sure he is not Korean.' In this situation, (8) has an implicit involvement with the conscious participant.

(8) *kare   wa   nihonzin   da*
    he   TOP   Japanese.person   COP
    'He is Japanese.'

(9) *kare   wa   tabun   nihonzin   da.*
    he   TOP   possibly   Japanese.person   COP
    'He is possibly Japanese.'

(10) *kare   wa   nihonzin   da   to   omou.*
     he   TOP   Japanese.person   COP   COMP   think
     'I think he is Japanese.'

In Section 4.2, I argue that the speaker involvement proposed by Maat and Degand is not the only way in which the speaker is involved in construing a causal relationship. I will demonstrate those elements of speaker involvement specific to the original type of speaker involvement in Section 4.2.2. Then, in Section 4.2.3, another type of speaker involvement will be introduced. Section 4.2.4 will show how all of the usages of *kara* discussed in this book can be captured with these two speaker involvement scales.

4.2.2 The first speaker involvement scale

It must be pointed out that all four factors that are used to measure 'speaker involvement,' as proposed by Maat and Degand (2001), have to do with perspectives.

The first factor of the speaker involvement explained in [1] is used to check whether there is a conscious participant (i.e., a protagonist or a speaker) in the expression whose perspective is going to be utilized by a speaker. Additionally, the other factors explained in [2], [3], and [4] indicate the strength of the perspectives of the speaker and the protagonist.

My interpretation is that the speaker involvement scale by Maat and Degand measures the extent to which the speaker is involved in detecting and reporting causation using these perspectives. In non-volitional content reading, no perspective is involved in causation. The speaker can detect causation without referring to perspectives. In volitional content reading, the speaker has to infer the protagonist's state of mind in order to find the link between the intention of the protagonist and the action.[32] That is, the speaker must take the protagonist's perspective and in doing so the speaker is more involved in detecting causation than in non-volitional content reading. Finally, it is the speaker's own perspective that creates the link between cause and effect in the case of epistemic and speech act readings. The speaker is the only person who can detect and report the relationships to then detect or report causation. Causation is ordered, as mentioned above, in terms of increasing speaker involvement: non-volitional content reading, volitional content reading, epistemic reading, and speech act reading.

In this section, the term 'perspective' is used in a broader sense than in Chapter 2, where it referred to the deictic center of tense and epistemic modality. I assume that the latter focuses on a specific aspect of the former.

Let us look back at the analysis in Chapter 2 from the point of view of subject involvement. In Chapter 2, I analyzed three types of sentences. First, volitional content[33] and epistemic readings were contrasted. Then, volitional content and SAC (content reading with special access to cause) were contrasted.

The analysis of the first two readings in Chapter 2 shows that in the case of volitional content readings, the speaker cannot directly access the cause but has to use the protagonist's point of view, while in the case of the epistemic reading, the speaker can access the cause. With the notion of speaker involvement, this analysis can be taken to indicate that the latter has higher speaker involvement than the former. This observation is consistent with and can been seen as a specific case of the analysis by Maat and Degand.

The issue now is where on the scale SAC can be placed. In this type, the tense is suspended in the dependent clause and expresses special access to cause, by either the protagonist (SAC-1), or the speaker (SAC-2). See Section 2.3.1.2 for more details about SAC.

Example (11) is a SAC sentence in which the protagonist has special access to the cause, called SAC-1.

(11) SAC-1
kodomo ga naku kara Yoko wa omotya o kat-ta.
child NOM cry because Yoko TOP toy ACC buy-PAST
'Yoko bought a toy for her child because of her child's crying.'

While this sentence reports the same events as (4), the protagonist's involvement in the relationship is different. As discussed in 2.3.1.2 in (11), cause and effect are less separable in nature compared to (4). In (11), how the protagonist perceives the cause is realized as an action of the protagonist. The action of buying a toy shows how the protagonist felt when she saw her child crying.

Since it shows the perspective of the protagonist, volitional content is the closest to SAC-1 among the causal relations examined in Maat and Degand (2001). SAC-1 also resembles non-volitional content in the sense that the cause and effect are less separable compared to volitioinal content. In this book, I will order SAC-1 between volitional and non-volitional content relations.

Let us continue on to SAC-2 and examine the sentence in (12).

(12) SAC-2
    issyokenmei   benkyoosuru kara   kare wa   karada o
    with.all.energy study   because he   TOP   health ACC
    kowasi-ta.
    ruin-PAST
    'He ruined his health because of studying too hard.'

SAC-2 shows the access of the speaker to the cause, while expressing a relation between the events. Usually, when causals express causation between events (that is, when the sentence expresses a content relation in a broad sense), the speaker cannot access the cause as disoussed in 2.3.3. However, in this sentence, the speaker's mental attitude toward the cause (i.e., accusation) is implied. This makes SAC-2 special: SAC-2 has features of both content and epistemic relations. We are going to locate SAC-2 close to epistemic relations among content relations on the speaker involvement scale.

4.2.3 The second speaker involvement scale

The *kara* sentences that I analyzed in Chapter 3 show various degrees of speaker involvement that do not necessarily have to do with reporting causation. To capture the speaker involvement observed in Chapter 3, I will propose another way to measure speaker involvement.

The speaker involvement scale proposed by Maat and Degand (2001), which I am going to call SIS-1, measures how the speaker is involved in detecting and reporting an event with perspectives. In my proposed second speaker involvement scale (SIS-2), the speaker is involved in constructing the relations that are reported with the sentence (See also Section 3.5).

In Chapter 3, it was argued that *kara* sentences can express static relations in addition to causation. Typical examples of *kara* sentences, such as (1) to (4), are based on causal laws. For example, the sentence in (1) reports a particular realization of a causal law as shown in (13).

(13) Causal law
ookaze   ga   huku   to   ki   ga   taoreru
strong.wind NOM   blow   whenever   tree   NOM   fall.down
'Whenever a strong wind blows, a tree falls down.'

On the other hand, static *kara* sentences (*kara* sentences that express static relations) are based on association.[34] The sentence in (14) is an example of a static *kara* sentence.

(14) Static
kanozyo   wa   nihonzin   da   kara   utikida. [with prejudice]
she   TOP   Japanese.person   COP   because   be.shy
'She is shy because she is Japanese.'

If the speaker meets a few Japanese people, all of whom happen to be shy, then, without any theoretical backup, the speaker may begin to associate being Japanese with being shy. The sentence in (14) reports a particular instance of an association such as (15):

(15) Association
nihonzin   wa   utikina   mono   da.
Japanese.person   TOP   be.shy   thing   COP
'Japanese are shy.'

In many static *kara* sentences such as (15), the contingency of the associated units is regarded as imperfect. One may or may not have the association between the units when the link is imperfect. Therefore, when the speaker uses the sentence in (14), it is implied that the speaker has an association such as (15) in mind. It displays the speaker's intentionality. On the other hand, causal laws are based on perfect contingency. No intentionality of the speaker is displayed. The completeness of the contingency is the continuity behind causal law and association. As the completeness of this relationship lessens, the speaker's involvement in relating the events increases.

Here is another example of a static *kara* sentence.

(16) Static

> sora ga aoi kara kanasii
> sky NOM be.blue because be.sad
> 'I'm sad because the sky is blue.'

This sentence reports a particular realization of association as follows.

(17) Association

> sora ga aoi to kanasii mono da.
> sky NOM be.blue whenever be.sad thing COP
> 'Whenever the sky is blue, I'm sad.'

The association in (17) is more private than that in (15). That is, the speaker involvement of (16) is higher than in (14) in relation to SIS-2.

Static *kara* sentences based on imperfect contingencies have a higher level of speaker involvement than either dynamic *kara* sentences or static *kara* sentences with perfect contingency with respect to SIS-2. Even static *kara* sentences with perfect contingency have higher speaker involvement than dynamic *kara* sentences with respect to SIS-2, because the association is based on the knowledge of the speaker, while causal law belongs to the world.

Whether a *kara* sentence is static or dynamic depends on the knowledge of the speaker. If the speaker knows that there is a causal relationship between the season autumn and leaves turning yellow, the sentence in (18) is dynamic. On the other hand, if the speaker regards leaves turning yellow as only one of a number of aspects of autumn, this sentence is a static causal.

(18) Static/Dynamic

> aki da kara ha ga irozuku.
> autumn COP because leaf NOM turn.yellow
> 'The leaves are turning yellow because it is autumn.'

In SIS-2, as the detection of causation is attenuated, the speaker's involvement increases. Instead of using the objective relationships of causal law as the basis for reporting a relationship, the knowledge of the speaker is utilized.

There are static *kara* causals that seem to have higher speaker involvement with respect to SIS-1 compared to the static sentence in (14). These were called epistemic and speech act static *kara* sentences in Chapter 3. Here are some examples.

(19) Static epistemic
    kare wa   oyakookooda   kara   erai.
    he   TOP be.thoughtful.towards.parents because be.honorable
    'He is honorable, because he thinks about his parents.'

Dynamic content reports a particular instance of a causal law. Dynamic epistemic content expresses inference based on a causal law. While both are based on causal law, there is a big difference between the two readings. In contrast, static epistemic and static content are both particular instances of association. Therefore, the distinction between content and epistemic readings is not as essential in the case of static readings as it is for dynamic readings. However, we are going to distinguish between these two categories because static epistemic resembles dynamic epistemic in the sense that the apodosis seems to express the speaker's epistemic state. This is because, among the associations, the one that associates something with the speaker's evaluation underlies static epistemic.

Let us move on to the static speech act.

(20) Static speech act
    otoko da   kara   naka-nai-de
    man COP because cry-NEG(IMP)
    'You shouldn't cry (=Please don't cry), because you are a man.'

Examples of static speech acts are rare and many of them are idiomatic. Static speech act *kara* sentences express speech acts based on association.

4.2.4 Categorizing sentences with two scales

The following figure shows the relationship between the SISs and various relations expressed with *kara* sentences.

SIS-1 measures how the speaker is involved in detecting and reporting a relationship. When the speaker involvement is extremely high with respect to

```
                              SIS-1
                               ▲
                               │
                    ┌─── Dynamic ──── ···· Static ············
                    │                                         :
                    │   Speech act        (Static speech act) :
Speaker's perspective│                                        :
                    │   Epistemic         (Static epistemic)  :
                    │  ···Content···                          :
                    │   :         :                           :
                    │   : SAC-2   :                           :
Protagonist's perspective         :                           :
                    │   : Volitional                          :
                    │   :         :                           :
                    │   : SAC-1   :                           :
                    │   :         :                           :
   No perspective   │   Non-volitional    Static content      :
                    │   :         :                           :
                    └───·········─·········──────────────────·┘
                    └──────────┬────────┘└────────┬─────────┘   ▶ SIS-2
                          Causation       Based on association by the speaker
                                          ⎧                              ⎫
                                   ←── Perfect contingency   Imperfect contingency ──→
```

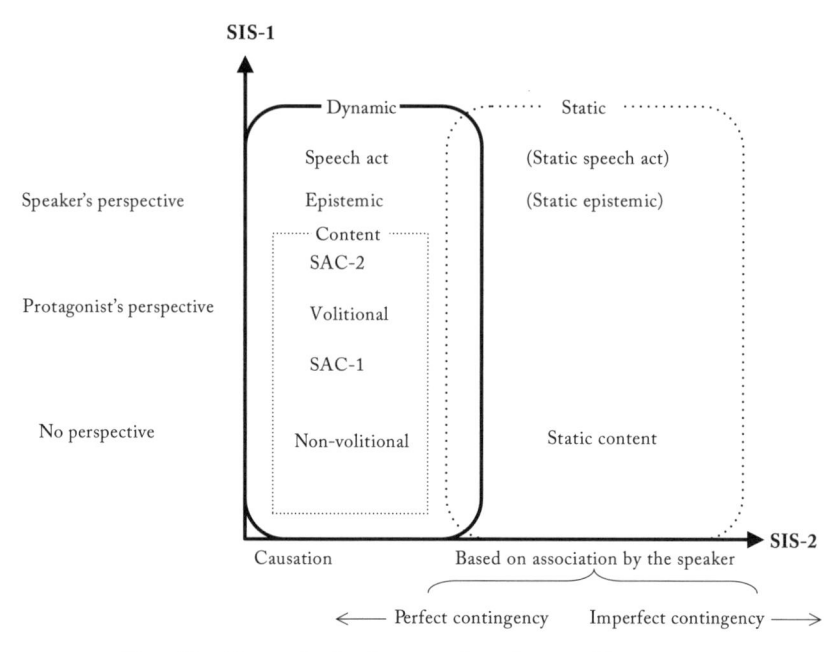

Figure 4.1 Two speaker involvement scales and usages of *kara* sentences

SIS-1, the speaker becomes a referent of the causal sentence. How the speaker uses the perspectives defines how the speaker is involved in the relationship.

On the other hand, SIS-2 measures how the speaker is involved in constructing the relationship that is reported with causal sentences. The speaker is highly involved when the reported relationship is based on association with an imperfect contingency and displays the speaker's intentionality. Even in this case, since it is not the association itself that is going to be reported, the speaker does not become a part of the referent. As detection of causation becomes difficult between the units connected with *kara*, the speaker's association between the units is used.

I have explored the relationship between content and epistemic readings. Figure 4.1 shows that these are connected in numerous ways. First, I pointed out that content readings in Sweetser (1990) have various subtypes: ordinary content, SAC-1, and SAC-2. Ordinary content can be divided into two types: volitional and non-volitional. I used volitional content as the typical content causal in Chapter 2 in order to observe the perspective structure. With respect to SIS-1, SAC-2 comes between volitional content and epistemic readings. Moreover, SAC-1 comes between volitional and non-volitional readings. Turning to SIS-2, static content seems to fall somewhere between content and epistemic readings on the continuum, as it expresses a relation between the content domains, but reflects the speaker's knowledge. My explanation is that it reflects the speaker knowledge, but in a different way to the dynamic epistemic reading.[35]

4.3 Analysis of *kara* and *node*

In this section, I will show that analysis using the two speaker involvement scales can be useful through the analysis of one of the most famous problems in Japanese linguistics: the distinction between the two causal connectives, *kara* and *node*.

4.3.1 Two competing theories
4.3.1.1 Mainstream analysis
There has been a great deal of research that has discussed the differences in the usage of *kara* and *node*. The widely accepted distinction between the two (e.g., Iwasaki 1995; Nagano, 1952, 1988; see also Higashiizumi, 2006, for a recent review) can be rephrased using Sweetser's categorizations: *node* can be used in dynamic content readings but, in most cases, it is difficult to use it in dynamic epistemic and dynamic speech act readings. Let us verify this observation with examples.

The naturalness of the sentence in (21), with both *node* and *kara*, show that both connectives can be used for content readings.

(21) Dynamic content
    ame ga   hut-ta   {kara /node} zimen ga   nure-ta
    rain NOM fall-PAST because   ground NOM get.wet-PAST
    'The ground got wet because it rained.'

As the examples in (22) and (23) show, *kara* can be used for dynamic epistemic and dynamic speech act, but *node* is restricted in its usage.

(22) Dynamic epistemic
    kare wa paatii ga   suki {da kara / *na node} paatii ni
    he   TOP party NOM love COP because   party LOC

> iku daroo.
> go must
> 'He must be going to the party, because he loves parties.'

(23) Dynamic speech act
> abunai   {kara / *node}   atti   ni   it-te-nasai.
> be.dangerous because   overt.there   LOC   go (IMP)
> 'Go away, because this place is dangerous.'

As we have already seen in Section 4.2.1, Maat and Degand (2001) have pointed out that subject involvement increases with respect to SIS-1 in the following order: content, epistemic, and speech act readings. This means that the previous analysis in Japanese linguistics of *node* can be interpreted as indicating that *node* is restricted in its appearance when there is a high speaker involvement with respect to SIS-1.

Let's see the behavior of *node* in volitional content and SAC sentences.
For volitional content readings, both *kara* and *node* can be used, as shown in (24).

(24) Volitional content reading
> kodomo ga   nai-ta   {kara / node} Yoko   wa   omotya o
> child NOM   cry-PAST   because   Yoko   TOP   toy   ACC
> kat-ta.
> buy-PAST
> 'Yoko bought a toy for her child because her child cried.'

Moving to the SAC type, (25) shows that both kara and *node* can be used in SAC-1.[36]

(25) SAC-1
> kodomo ga   naku   {kara / node} Yoko   wa   omotya o
> child NOM   cry   because   Yoko   TOP   toy   ACC
> kat-ta.
> buy-PAST
> 'Yoko bought a toy for her child because of her child's crying.'

On the other hand, *node* cannot be used for SAC-2, while *kara* can. The *node* sentence in (26) is unnatural.

(27) SAC-2
 isssyokenmei *benkyoosuru* {*kara* / *node} *kare* *wa* *karada*
 with.all.energy study because he TOP health
 o *kowasi-ta*
 ACC ruin-PAST
 'He ruined his health because of studying too hard.'

The following table summarizes the observations in Section 4.2.1. In this table, 'OK' means that the connective can express the relation; 'R' means that the connective is restricted in expressing the relation.

Table 4.1 Usages of *node* with respect to SIS-1

Subject involvement with respect to SIS-1	Relations		Occurrence of node
High	Speech act		R
↑	Epistemic		R
	Content	SAC-2	R
		Volitional	OK (See Section 4.3.3)
↓		SAC-1	OK
Low		Non-volitional	OK

4.3.1.2 Analysis by Miyagawa and Nakamura (1991)

The problem with the analysis we have seen in the previous section is that it is impossible to explain the observation made by Miyagawa and Nakamura (1991) on the following examples (from Miyagawa & Nakamura (1991:435)):

(27) *Hanako* *wa* *hahanohi* {*da kara* / *na node*} *akai* *kaaneesyon*
 Hanako TOP Mother's Day COP because red carnation
 o *age-ta*.
 ACC give-PAST
 'Hanako gave (her mother) red carnations because it was Mother's Day.'

For clarity, I will call these sentences that use causal connectives to express the relationship between Hanako's gift of red carnations to her mother, and it being Mother's Day, 'carnation sentences.' Miyagawa and Nakamura point out that, in (27), when *node* is used, it reports necessary causation. That is, it is necessary for the act of giving the carnations to her mother to be followed by the fact that it is Mother's Day. They suggest that this sentence implies that it is a tradition to give red carnations on Mother's Day, and that the sentence reports that Hanako followed this tradition. On the other hand, by using *kara* in (27), this sentence expresses the action of Hanako as a phenomenon. Using the terms proposed by Goldsmith and Woisetschlaeger (1982), they point out that *node* expresses structural knowledge and *kara* expresses phenomenal knowledge.

There are, however, many examples that cannot be explained with this analysis. First of all, there are sentences such as that shown in (28), which express structural knowledge, but in which both *node* and *kara* are possible.

(28) *umi ga   tikai {kara / node} romantikkuda.*
      sea NOM close because   be.romantic
      'It is romantic because the sea is nearby.'

In addition, there are cases such as (29). This shows structural knowledge, yet *node* cannot be used while *kara* can.

(29) *iiko   {da kara / *na node} sizukani si-nasai.*
      good.boy COP because   be.quiet do (IMP)
      'You shoud be quiet (=Please be quiet), because you are a good boy.'

Moreover, it is difficult to explain the distribution of *kara* and *node* shown in the previous section with these two types of knowledge. Neither of the theories presented in 4.3.1 is enough to explain the distribution of the two causal connectives. In Sections 4.3.2-4.3.4, I will show that, by using the two speaker involvement scales, it is possible to explain all the examples shown in Section 4.3.1 in a coherent way.

4.3.2 SIS-2 and *node* sentences

Here, the observation by Miyagawa and Nakamura is interpreted as follows. First, if we use *node* in (27), the speaker involvement is high with respect to SIS-2 and it becomes an example of a static causal. (27) with *node* expresses a particular instance of association, which is given in (30):

(30) *hahanohi   ni wa   okaasan ni   akai kaaneesyon o   ageru*
    Mother's Day at TOP mother DAT red carnation ACC give
    mono[37] *da.*
    thing COP
    'Mother's Day is a day when people give red carnations to their mothers.'

On the other hand, when *kara* is used in the same sentence in (27), the speaker involvement becomes lower than in the case when *node* is used with respect to SIS-2. It reports force dynamics in the content level. Once SIS-2 is adopted, the observation by Miyagawa and Nakamura is no longer isolated. Let us determine where the relationships expressed by the sentences in (27) are located on the SIS-2 scale.

To begin with, typical causal sentences such as (1) are based on causal laws (i.e., perfectly contingent relationships) and sentences such as (13) are located in the lowest position on SIS-2. In the same way, when the carnation sentence in (27) is used with *kara*, it is based on a causal law. Since this sentence has volitional content, it has higher speaker involvement with respect to SIS-1 than non-volitional content such as (1). However, they both have the same level of speaker involvement with respect to SIS-2. The fact that it is Mother's Day is Hanako's motivation, which is translated into her action of giving carnations to her mother. This relationship between motivation and action is sustained by a causal law. When the carnation sentence in (27) is used with *node*, it has a slightly higher speaker involvement than when it is used with *kara*. This time, between it being Mother's Day and giving carnations, there is an association, as shown in (30). Miyagawa and Nakamura called this a tradition to indicate that the association is shared by many people. The fact that the speaker bears this relation in mind is not prominent. In the case of (14), however, the sentence is based on an association known as prejudice, such as that given in (15). As we can argue that the relationship between being Japanese and being shy is not necessarily the case, this prejudice is not widely shared by many people compared to traditional associations. As a result, the speaker's state of mind stands out. Lastly, private associations, such as that in (17), which is behind the static sentence in (16), are shared with almost no one and the fact that the speaker has such an association stands out. That is, speaker involvement is extremely high with respect to SIS-2. In brief, speaker involvement gets higher in the order of (1) and (27) with *kara*, (27) with *node*, (14) and (16). Various relationships in SIS-2 are shown in Figure 4.2.

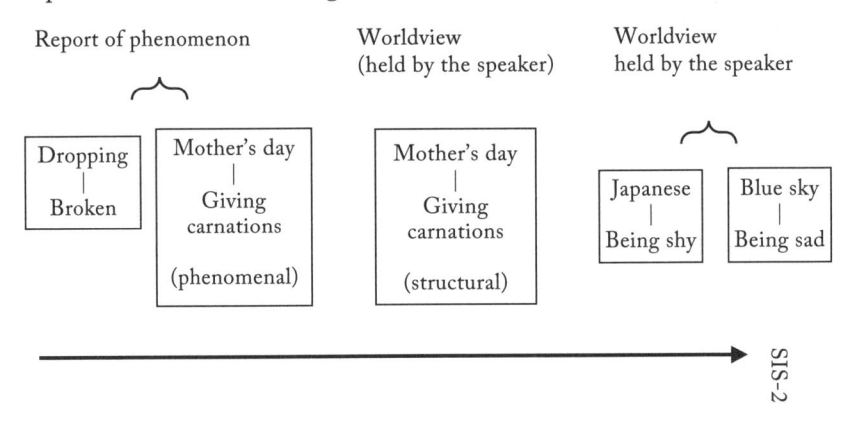

Figure 4.2　Various relationships in SIS-2

By only looking at phenomenal knowledge and structural knowledge, it is very difficult to say which is more subjective. The adoption of SIS-2 enables us to say that a specific type of speaker involvement or subjectivity is higher in structural knowledge than in phenomenal knowledge.

The advantage of using SIS-2 is not only that we can compare and categorize examples, but also that we can explain why the carnation sentence with *node* expresses a static relation while the carnation sentence with *kara* expresses a dynamic relation. This point will be elaborated on in 4.3.4 but, before that, the relationship between volition and SIS-1 must be analyzed.

4.3.3 SIS-1 and volitional content reading

The volition of the protagonist is the crucial factor in analyzing the carnation sentence. There are many causal relations that are ambiguous in their level of volition. (31) gives an example of this.

(31) *ame   ga   hut-ta   kara   kare wa   dekake-nakat-ta.*
　　 rain NOM fall.down-PAST because he   TOP go.out-NEG-PAST
　　 'He didn't go out because it rained.'

When the *kara* sentence in (31) means that he did not feel like going out because of the rain, it expresses a volitional relation. If it means that he could not go out for some physical reason, it is an example of a less volitional relation. For example, if he had injured his leg, making it impossible for him to go out in the rain, then the sentence expresses a less volitional relation.

As Maat and Degand (2001) have pointed out, a volitional causal relationship has a higher speaker involvement than a non-volitional relation with respect to SIS-1. Thus, a less volitional sentence can be located between typically volitional and typically non-volitional sentences.

Since the usage of *node* is restricted in high SIS-1, it is possible to hypothesize that *node* is inclined towards low speaker involvement in SIS-1. Under this condition, it can be predicted that, if we use *node*, the sentence tends to express a less volitional relation than *kara* when the sentence is ambiguous between volitional and less volitional relations.

I can use this hypothesis to explain a well-known contrast between *kara* and *node*. In Japanese, (32) with *node* is preferred to (32) with *kara* in offering an excuse for arriving late; (32) with *kara* sounds rude, and (32) with *node* sounds polite (Nagano, 1952). This sentence is ambiguous between a volitional relation and a less volitional relation. I believe that this is because when the sentence takes the strongly volitional reading, it implies that the protagonist was able to avoid being late and this leads to it sounding rude. On the other hand, when the sentence has a less volitional reading, the sentence implies that being late was unavoidable, and thus, the statement sounds polite.

(32) *neboosi-ta* {*kara* /*node*} *okure-masi-ta.*
 get.up.late-PAST because get.late (POL)-PAST
 'I was late because I got up late.'

If we hypothesize the inclination of *node* to lower SIS-1, we can explain the distribution as follows: in *kara* sentences, we cannot avoid volitional readings, but in *node* sentences less-volitional readings are preferred and so a difference in politeness occurs.

4.3.4 Solution with the two speaker involvement scales

The analyses given in Sections 4.3.2 and 4.3.3 are prerequisites for the analysis of the carnation sentence in (27). Here is the sentence again.

(33) (= (27))
Hanako wa hahanohi {da kara / na node} akai kaaneesyon o
Hanako TOP Mother's Day COP because red carnation ACC
age-ta.
give-PAST
'Hanako gave (her mother) red carnations because it was Mother's Day.'

This sentence is also ambiguous between volitional and less volitional relations. When this sentence takes a strongly volitional reading and there is a causal relationship between the motivation and the act, we can easily see the relationship between it being Mother's Day and giving carnations. On the other hand, if we take a less volitional reading, it is difficult to find a causal relation between the events. This is the case when Hanako could not avoid giving carnations. For this sentence, it is difficult to find a less volitional causal law that is applicable between Hanako's present and it being Mother's Day. As I argued in characterizing SIS-2 in Sections 4.2.3 and 4.2.4, in this case, since the detection of causation is weak, the speaker's knowledge has to be utilized to associate the protasis and the apodosis. This results in a static reading of the *node* sentence in (27).

When a sentence is ambiguous between a volitional relation and a less volitional relation, I assume that, comparing *node* to *kara*, allows it to take a less volitional reading because *node* has an inclination to lower SIS-1 (Section 4.3.3). When the sentence is read with a less volitional reading, it is sometimes difficult to find a causal relation between the two events. In this case, it is interpreted that the speaker connected the two events with association, which results in a static reading. When there is no possibility of connecting the sentence with causation, as in the case of (34), the sentence takes a static reading whether the connective is *node* or *kara*.

(34) umi ga tikai {kara / node} romantikkuda.
sea NOM close because be.romantic
'It is romantic because the sea is nearby.'

I propose that a *node* sentence has an inclination to express lower subject involvement in SIS-1 in contrast to *kara*. This can be observed when the relationship itself is ambiguous between volitional and less volitional relations. In this case, the contrast between *kara* and *node* becomes clearer compared to other cases. When the relationship is less volitional, it is sometimes difficult to find the causal relationship that connects the two events. When causal laws are hard to detect, causal sentences are interpreted as based on the association of the speaker. In this case, the subject involvement is higher in SIS-2. This is the explanation that can be provided through the use of the two SISs, in addition to an assumption about the nature of *node* in relation to the behavior in the carnation sentences. This is why, in the carnation sentences, *node* sentences express a static relation. However, *node* sentences do not always have higher subject involvement. It is only the interaction between the two scales that allows for this analysis.

4.3.5 Reanalyzing Nagano's (1988) data

Nagano (1988) asked 683 people to complete sentences, such as the following, with either *kara* or *node*.

(35) *abunai   (   )   atti e   it-te-nasai.*
    be.dangerous because over.there   go (IMP)
    'Go away, because this place is dangerous.'

(36) *hazimete   hikooki   ni   not-ta   ga,   angai   yurenai*
    first.time airplane LOC   ride-PAST   but   unexpectedly shake-NEG
    (   )   *ansinsi-ta.*
    because   be.relieved.
    'I got on a plane for the first time, and was relieved because there was no turbulence.'

Among Nagano's (1988) participants, 89.6% chose *kara* and only 0.7% chose *node* for (35). In contrast, for (36), only 0.9% of the participants chose *kara* and 84.8% chose *node*. Nagano argues that his claim (1952) that *kara* expresses a subjective relation, while *node* expresses an objective relation, is fully substantiated by these data. The contrast between (35) and (36) seems to support his claim. However, a problem arises in the contrast between (36) and (37).

(37) *koko wa   umi ga   tikai   (   )   kaze ga   suzusii.*
    here TOP sea NOM   be.close   because wind NOM   be.cool
    'The wind is cool because the sea is nearby.'

For (37), 15.7% chose *kara* and 23.0 % chose *node*. In (36), the causation is between the airplane remaining stable and the feeling of relief. (37) expresses causation between closeness to the sea and the wind being cool. The causation in (36) includes the perspective of the speaker who is the protagonist, but the causation in (37) does not. Consequently, we may say that the relationship in (37) is more objective in Nagano's terms or has less speaker involvement with respect to SIS-1 than (36). For these examples, Nagano's (1952) hypothesis does not make a correct prediction: *node* was used more often in (36) than in (37).

My analysis can be applied to explain the contrast between (36) and (37). Note that the sentence in (36) has a protagonist (the speaker himself) and is ambiguous between volitional and less volitional relations without a specific causal connective. I posit that, since a less volitional reading is proper for this sentence, many people chose *node*. Nagano's theory predicts that *kara* does not occur when the sentence expresses a relation with low speaker involvement with respect to SIS-1. In my analysis, *kara* can occur in low SIS-1, and it correctly predicts that, in (36), the relationship has low SIS-1 and both *kara* and *node* are chosen by native speakers.

4.4 Theoretical contributions to Japanese linguistics: Two levels of subjectivity

Below, I will show that the notion of subjectivity concerning *kara* sentences in Japanese linguistics can be clarified with analyses that use the two SISs.

Nagano (1952) has argued that *node* marks an objective relationship and *kara* marks a subjective relationship. Kunihiro (1992) argued the reverse; that is, *kara* is objective and *node* is subjective. It would seem that these two native speakers came to opposite conclusions because the notion of speaker involvement was not clear.

It should be noted that, in some places in their arguement, both *node* and *kara* are characterized in a more complicated way. Nagano claims that *node* expresses objective relations objectively. See (38):

(38) Nagano (1952)
These examples all <u>describe phenomena or events that are above subjectivity</u> $_{(a)}$, and <u>describe the objective relations as they are</u> $_{(b)}$. (Characterization

of *node*)

Additionally, Nagano characterizes *kara* as a causal connective that expresses subjective phenomena subjectively. (a) has to do with how the world is constructed, and (b) has to do with how the speaker expresses the world.

The problem with this characterization is that he assumes that (a) and (b) always take the same value. When (a) is subjective, (b) is also subjective. Logically, there should be four types of connectives if we take (a) and (b) separately. In my analysis, it is possible to describe four semantic categories of causal connectives. In this framework, subjectivity in (a) is scaled with SIS-2, and subjectivity in (b) is scaled with SIS-1.

Let us start from (a). When a relation is extremely subjective with respect to SIS-2, then we have a static reading. When it is extremely objective with respect to SIS-2, we have a dynamic reading. Moving to (b), when a relation is extremely subjective with respect to SIS-1, then we have epistemic and speech act readings, plus SAC-2. In addition, when it is extremely objective with respect to

Table 4.2 Subjectivity, objectivity, and *kara*

(Constructing the relation, Reporting the releation)	*Nagano's analysis*	*The analysis of* kara *in this book*
(Objective, Objective)	(*node*)	Dynamic ordinary content, SAC-1
(Objective, Subjective)	N/A	SAC-2, Dynamic epistemic, Dynamic speech act
(Subjective, Objective)	N/A	Static content
(Subjective, Subjective)	*kara*	Static epistemic, Static speech act

SIS-1, we have content readings, including SAC-1. These four categories are summarized in the following table.

I would like to reevaluate the analysis by Nagano, since it has pointed out that how the speaker understands causation is essential in analyzing causal connectives, and additionally implies that there are two different levels of subjectivity related to causal connectives.

My analysis expands this on two points. First, I clearly characterize the two different levels of subjectivity. Second, I adopt a scalar approach in analyzing the two levels of subjectivity. Compared to the binary analysis, which only asks whether the relation is subjective or not, my analysis can deal with various relations, as shown in Table 4.2.

4.5 Conclusions

By assessing how the speaker is involved in an expressed relation, I analyzed both *kara* sentences and *node* sentences. Two relations between the speaker and causation were shown: [1] How we construct perspective structures in reporting causation, and [2] The display of intentionality that underlies causation. It is argued that this approach reveals the continuity between discrete relations, such as content, epistemic, and speech act readings.

This chapter has proposed an analysis based on how[38] the speaker interacts with the events. Recently many studies have successfully observed the emergence of categories using robots or computerized agents. As the robots or agents are only assigned a simple body or sensory-motor system, the categorizations are a direct result of how they use their body to interact with the environment. This type of categorization is referred to as 'dynamical categorization' by Morimoto and Ikegami (2004) (See also Uno & Ikegami, 2005, for an analysis from a linguistic point of view). For example, some robots categorize the shape or size of objects based on how they grasp them (Marocco & Floreano, 2002; Scheier & Pfeifer, 1995). Other robots categorize the shape of objects or rooms by the way the agents move (Morimoto & Ikegami, 2004; Tani & Nolfi, 1998). There is an agent that categorizes the speed of lights flashing on and off based on the way the agent approaches the light (Iizuka & Ikegami, 2004). The categories generated in these studies are radial rather than classical (in the sense of Lakoff, 1987).

My analysis of *kara* sentences, in a broad sense, can also be seen as an example of dynamical categorization. The analysis is based on how the speaker interacts with the world, and results in a radial category, as shown in Figure 4.1. The importance of embodiment in language has been emphasized in cognitive linguistics (Ikegami & Zlatev, 2008; Lakoff & Johnson, 1980, 1999; Zlatev, 2002). Analysis using SISs provides a way of linking the origins of grammar and embodiment.

Chapter 5

Joint attention and grammar

5.1 Introduction

In the previous chapter, I developed the analysis in cognitive linguistics with two speaker involvement scales (SIS). SIS-1 has to do with how a speaker's perspective is related with detection of causation. In contrast, SIS-2 measures the speaker's involvement in the existence of the relation that is expressed with causals.

To utter sentences with high speaker involvement in SIS-2 is to show that the speaker's consciousness is directed to a certain relationship. In this chapter, I explore how the display of the speaker's intentionality (i.e. the direction of consciousness) works in interaction. I propose that the display of the speaker's intentionality can lead the speaker to share intentionality with the hearer. Below, I will apply the notion 'joint attention' in developmental psychology to analyze the relationship between the speaker, the hearer and static *kara* sentences.

Section 5.2 points out that the motivation for uttering static *kara* sentences has to be inquired. Furthermore, it suggests that the extended notion of joint attention must give us a clue in determining motivation for static *kara* sentences. Section 5.3 explains the original notion of joint attention in psychology. Section 5.4 extends the notion of joint attention and uses it to analyze static *kara* sentences. Section 5.5 explores the possibility of grounding this argument thus far with respect to conventional linguistics. Section 5.6 concludes the argument.

By taking interaction into view, the two speaker involvement scales can be interpreted by a hearer as follows: SIS-1 is related with hearer's detecting the perspective of the speaker, and SIS-2 is related with the hearer's sharing the perspective with the speaker.

5.2 Unsolved problems with static *kara* sentences

In Chapter 3, I pointed out that sentences with causal connectives can express static relations: particular instances of association. For example, see (1):

(1) *aki   da   kara   simizimisuru ne.*
    autumn COP because feel.lonely   FP
    'I feel lonely because it is autumn.'

The sentence is based on an association, such as (2):

(2) *aki   wa   simizimisuru mono da*
    autumn TOP   feel.lonely thing COP
    (*to   watasi wa   omou*).
    (COMP   I   TOP   think)
    '(I think that) autumn is a time when people feel lonely.'

In (2), it is possible to attach *to watasi wa omou* 'I think that,' which shows that the association shown in (2) is imperfectly contingent. In this chapter, I will focus only on static causals based on imperfect contingency.

An ordinary causal sentence such as (3) expresses a causal and temporal relation that is based on a causal law, while a static causal sentence such as (1) expresses a non-causal and spatial relationship (Uno, 2006).

(3) *ookaze   ga   hui-ta   kara   ki   ga   taore-ta.*
    strong.wind NOM blow-PAST because tree NOM fall.down-PAST
    'The tree fell down because a strong wind blew.'

Some features of static causal sentences are unexplained in Chapter 3 and in Uno (2006).

To begin with, static causals based on imperfect contingency are not informative,[39] as pointed out in Section 3.5.2. Association with imperfect contingency is not necessarily shared in the society. Then, the fact that at least the speaker bears such a contingency in mind will be highlighted. The report of a realization of imperfect contingency, such as (1), does not give reliable information about the world. Instead, it implies how the speaker conceives the world, as shown in (2). This raises the following question: what is the motivation of uttering non-informative sentences?

Secondly, what is the difference between uttering a static causal and explicitly mentioning the association behind it? For example, what is the difference between uttering (1) and uttering (2)?

My hypothesis is that static causals can be used to achieve intersubjectivity between the speaker and the hearer, while ordinary dynamic causals are used to transmit information. Intersubjectivity, or sharing intentionality, is argued to be a prerequisite for and the goal of interaction (Trevarthen, 1993) in developmental psychology. I hypothesize that in achieving intersubjectivity, (2), but not (1), can be used.

An expression that does not convey information is termed 'redundant' in this book. Many analyses of conversation or discourse focus on the redundant nature of language (e.g. Garrod & Pickering, 2004), with some exceptions (e.g. Groz & Sidner, 1986). On the other hand, in many grammatical analyses, including those in cognitive linguistics, it is often implicitly assumed that sentences are used to convey information. The aim of this chapter is to show that even from a grammatical analysis perspective, it is useful to take into consideration that sentences are not always optimized for conveying information. The interactive aspect, rather than the informative aspect, of language is related to static causals.

Since cognitive linguistics currently lacks a tool to deal with intentionality, I will adopt the notion of 'joint attention' from developmental psychology to analyze static causals. Joint attention is a mechanism for sharing intentionality by using a triadic relationship between two persons and an object.

5.3 Joint attention in developmental psychology

Proto-linguistic communication, such as pointing or eye contact, develops at the age of 8 to 12 months. It is known that there are two types of proto-linguistic communication (Bates, 1976). The first type is called 'proto-imperative,' and it is a motion to make request to others. For example, it is known that children around this age tend to show their favorite toys to their caretakers by using pointing or eye contact (Baron-Cohen, Tager-Flusberg & Cohen, 1993, 2000). The second type is called 'proto-declarative,' and it is a motion to ask the caretaker to pay attention to some specific object. For example, when a child points out the moon to her mother, it does not mean the child wants the mother to fetch the moon. It often means that she wants her mother to see the moon.

Proto-declarative communication can only be achieved by human beings (Gómez, Sarria & Tamarit, 1993; Tomasello, 1999, 2003), and autistic children have difficulty in engaging in proto-declarative communication (Baron-Cohen, Tager-Flusberg & Cohen, 1993, 2000).

There are many attempts to explain the difference between these two types of proto-linguistic communication. Some researchers, most notably Baron-Cohen (1995), focused on a cognitive aspect. It was argued that the ability to manipulate meta-representation is required for proto-declaratives but not for proto-imperatives. Others such as Gómez, Sarria, and Tamarit (1993) focused on emotional and attentive aspects. They argued that in proto-imperatives, attention and emotion are means, and in proto-declaratives, attention and emotion are the goal for communication. Joint attention can be used to perform these two types of proto-linguistic communication.

Joint attention is the process of establishing a shared attention by showing an object or an event nonverbally using fingers or eyes. In Uno and Ikegami (2003, 2004), following the argument by Gómez, Sarria, and Tamarit, proto-imperative joint attention is called 'instrumental JA.' In this case, shared attention is used as a tool to achieve some goal. Moreover, proto-declarative joint attention is called 'participatory JA'. In this case, the joint attentive state itself becomes a goal of interaction.

Henceforth, I use the term joint attention with an extended meaning (also in Honda, 2005). Joint attention is a notion originally derived from developmental psychology, but I use this term in a broad sense. In an extended sense, joint attention refers to aligning the intentionality (the direction of consciousness) between two adults using language. In achieving extended joint attention, the third object is the notion expressed with language. The importance of joint attention in acquiring language is pointed out by Tomasello (1999, 2003) and others. However, in this chapter, the aim is to examine how the grammar of mature language and joint attention are related.

5.4 Extended notion of joint attention

5.4.1 Sharing intentionality using language

A one-word sentence is a kind of pointing, using a word instead of a finger or an eye movement. A noun can be used to direct attention to the object. In addition, since a person presents a word to the other person, uttering a one-word sentence to someone is more like establishing broadly conceived joint attention through words. Here is an example of a one-word sentence:

(4) *yuki.*
    snow
    Snow!

Onoe (1998, 2001) studied variations in one-word sentences and explained that two typical usages are requests and exclamations. When (4) is used as a request, it means "I want some snow!" When the same word is used to express exclamation it means "I'm moved by the snow!" He argues that a request reports the non-existence and an exclamation reports the existence of a thing.

While Onoe emphasizes that, fundamentally, one-word sentences are monologues that do not require a hearer, if they are spoken to other people, (4) as a request establishes an instrumental JA, and (4) as an exclamation establishes a participatory JA.

Below I will focus solely on the latter type; in the following sections, whenever I point to (4) I mean the one-word sentence in (4) with an exclamatory interpretation.

The one-word sentence in (4) expresses an exclamation towards the object. Only the name of the object is verbalized. The intended message of (4) is (5):

(5) *watasi   wa   yuki   ni   kandoosi-ta.*
    I   TOP   snow   DAT   be.moved-PAST
    'I'm moved by the snow!'

When the speaker utters (5) instead of (4), the speaker himself directs the attention of the hearer, and so the intentions of the speaker and the hearer will not be aligned. Thus, joint attention will not be established.

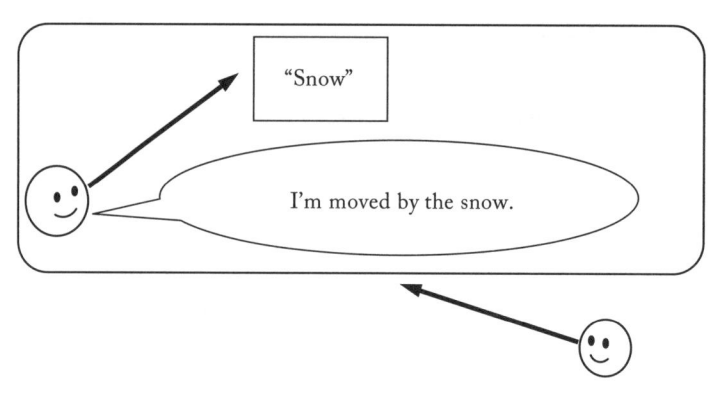

Figure 5.1 No joint attention

On the other hand, if the speaker lexicalize only the object that is in his consciousness as in (4), then the attention of the hearer will be given to that object. In this case, as shown in Figure 5.2, the intentionality of the speaker and the hearer will be aligned and joint attention will be established.

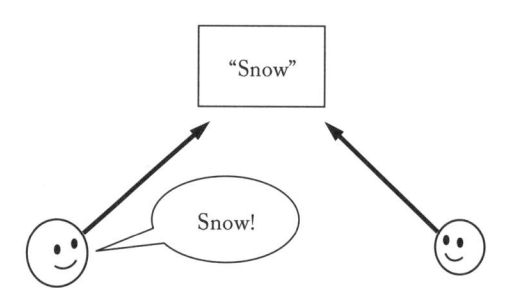

Figure 5.2 Joint attention

It is possible to say that a one-word sentence such as (4) expresses exclamation through the mechanism of joint attention. Under this assumption, I contend that in a participatory joint attentive linguistic expression, the discrepancy between what is expressed and how it is expressed is important. The subject's intention has to be expressed indirectly to establish joint attention.

To return to the problem of static causals: the characteristics that are pointed out in Section 5.2 can be explained by noting that static causals are used to establish participatory JA. See the following example:

(6) (=(1))
    aki   da   kara   simizimisuru ne.   [with exclamation]
    autumn COP because feel.lonely   FP
    'I feel lonely because it is autumn.'

While dynamic causals are used to transmit information, I propose that static causals such as (6) are used to achieve participatory JA between the speaker and the hearer. Just as with one-word sentences for exclamation, there is a discrepancy between the conveyed message (7) and what is verbalized (6):

(7) aki   wa   simizimisuru mono da   (to   watasi wa
    autumn TOP feel.lonely   thing COP (COMP I   TOP
    omou.)
    think)
    '(I think) autumn is a time when we feel lonely.'

If the speaker utters (7) instead of (6), the intentionality of the speaker and the hearer will not be shared, as shown in Figure 5.1. Only by uttering what is in the speaker's consciousness can the speaker and the hearer share intentionality, as shown in Figure 5.2. In this case, how the speaker conceives the relationship between autumn and loneliness is expressed not explicitly but implicitly in (6), demonstrating the speaker's intentionality.

5.4.2 Joint attention with and without grammar

While both (4) and (6) are sentences used to establish participatory JA, some differences can be pointed out.

Pointing using fingers or eyes and exclamative one-word sentences can be used only when the object that is pointed at or whose name is expressed is in front of the speaker. In this case, we can consider pointing to be dependent on the ground, and a one-word sentence is dependent on the ground of speech (Onoe, 2001). On the other hand, static causals are freer from the ground of speech, because what the speaker is going to present implicitly is an association: knowledge that belongs to the speaker. Because sentences that depend on grammar can convey complex relations, such as a particular realization of association, a joint attention that is independent of the situation is possible.

Not only the dependence on the context differs, but there is a difference in how they achieve joint attention. In (4), when a one-word sentence is used, the relationship between the speaker and the object triggers joint attention. There is an exclamation because the prediction towards the object turns out to be wrong (Michaelis & Lambrecht, 1996). More simply, the speaker is moved by the object (Onoe, 2001).

The static causal sentence in (6) represents ground-independent joint attention. Our ability to predict the minds of others is known as the 'theory of mind' (Baron-Cohen, Tager-Flusberg & Cohen, 1993; Premack & Woodruff, 1978). In interaction, people try to model other participants using predictions. It is easy to predict the behavior of a machine. However, since humans are autonomous, it is certainly impossible to make an accurate model. Therefore, the speaker and the hearer cannot fully predict each other in interaction (Ikegami, 2001; Uno & Ikegami, 2003). This can be the trigger for joint attention in this type of speech. The speaker attempts to draw the attention of the hearer to something other than themselves to maintain the ground of speech sound. A ground-independent joint attention can be established only with language and grammer.

Among two types of participatory JA, the one dependent on grammar assumes more involvement of the hearer, since the relationship between the speaker and the hearer is what triggers the establishment of joint attention.

5.5 Speech act theory and joint attention

Sentence types such as declaratives or exclamatives are defined as a conventionalized association of a communicative function (or a speech act) and a grammatical structure (Michaelis & Lambrecht, 1996). The two types of participatory JA which were presented in the previous section can be applied to analyze the relationship between exclamative and declarative sentences.

Onoe (2001) regards exclamative sentences as a direct extension of exclamative one-word sentences. In old Japanese, exclamative sentences were expressed with modified nouns with particles (Yamada, 1908, 1936).[40] As in the case of the one-word sentence in (4), the sentence in (8) only describes the object, while it conveys the exclamation of the speaker toward the object.

(8) *ahare uruhasiki tuki kana.*
    oh   beautiful moon FP
    'Oh, what a beautiful moon!'

Michaelis and Lambrecht (1996) point out that there is no unique form for expressing an exclamation in English. Intonation, inversion and several other techniques are used to express exclamation. Here is an example of an exclamative sentence in English. In (9), there is no element in the sentence that expresses explicitly that the speaker has an exclamation in mind. Rather, the relationship that caused the speaker's exclamation is described.[41]

(9) *She is* such *a good linguist!*

The sentences in (8) and (9) are both ground dependent. To interpret the sentence, one needs to refer to the ground of speech. In both cases the fact that the speaker is moved by a third object triggers the speech and, when the hearer is involved, participatory JA is achieved.

On the other hand, a ground-independent participatory JA, which can be achieved by sentence (6), can be realized with declarative sentences in general. A static causal sentence is just one example of such declarative sentences. As causals can be used in two ways, declarative sentences may be used for two functions: transmitting information and sharing intentionality.[42]

See the following sentence, which also establishes ground-independent participatory JA with redundant information. Instead of offering information, this type of declarative sentence can be used to share intentionality between the speaker and the hearer.

(10) *kyoo wa nitiyoobi da ne.*
     today TOP sunday COP FP
     'Today is Sunday.'

In this sentence, the intentionality of the speaker (which connects the subject and the predicate) is displayed. The motivation for uttering this sentence can be the relationship between the speaker and the hearer.

I assume that when a declarative sentence is uttered, we use a mental space structure to track the speaker's perspective, as an aid to understand the information the speaker is trying to convey. However, when the sentence is used to share intentionality, the detection of the mental space structure itself becomes the goal. This aspect is emphasized when the sentence lacks valuable information. Therefore, it may be said that redundancy or lack of information is not a necessary condition for participatory JA, but helps joint attention to occur when declarative sentences are used.

Sadock and Zwicky (1985) pointed out that exclamatives are closely related to declaratives. The analysis in this chapter adds weight to their observation. They explain the difference between exclamatives and declaratives as follows: '… in an exclamation, the speaker emphasizes his strong emotional reaction to what he takes to be a fact, whereas in a declarative, the speaker emphasizes his intellectual appraisal that the proposition is true.'

I have shown that [1] Both exclamatives and some declaratives can achieve participatory JA; and [2] The nature of joint attention is different between exclamatives and declaratives.[43]

5.6   Conclusions

In Section 5.2, I hypothesized that the function of static causals is not transmission of information, but rather sharing intentionality. The notion of participatory JA is adopted to determine the adequacy of this hypothesis. Under this hypothesis, it is possible to explain the difference between uttering a static causal and uttering the association behind the static causal. Only the former can achieve joint attention. It is a grammatically built-in tool for joint attention.

I proposed that it may be a characteristic of declarative sentences as a whole that *kara* can both transmit information and display intentionality to achieve participatory JA.

At a first glance, it seems strange that a special construction, such as causals, could have two different functions: namely, sharing intentionality and transmission of information. My assumption is that this comes from the features of declarative sentences; declarative sentences in general can have both functions. Moreover, features of static causals such as redundancy, interactivity, and implicitness in expressing subjectivity, can be explained as aspects of a form that is used to achieve participatory JA.

Recently, in evolutionary linguistics, there have been many attempts to explain how language, and especially complexity, has evolved (Hauser, Chomsky & Fitch, 2002; Pinker & Jackendoff, 2005; Steels, 2005). However, there have been not many attempts to look at how various types of sentences have evolved. The analysis in this section proposes the link between ground dependent and independent sentences and protolinguistic interaction.[44]

Chapter 6

Towards grammar from the first-person point of view

6.1 Analysis of *kara* sentences

Whether and how we can bridge between the cognition of what exists in the outer world and the cognition of one's own inner mind is always a problem in understanding consciousness in a scientific framework (Ikegami, 2000; Varela, 1992, etc.). Language seems to connect the two cognitions seamlessly. Alternatively, language may reflect the problem in a very intricate way so that we cannot easily recognize it. From this perspective, I have been interested in *kara* sentences. *Kara* sentences can express *both* speakers' minds and events happening in the world. I intend to reveal how content and epistemic readings are related. Content reading reports socio-physical causation and epistemic reading expresses the speaker's reasoning.

First, I extended the conventional analysis in cognitive/functional linguistics, exploring how form and meaning are linked differently in content and epistemic readings. A special type of content reading (SAC) has an irregular form/meaning linkage. I argued that perspective structures mediate the form and meaning of *kara* sentences. Only by referring to perspective structure can we analyze SAC and ordinary content and epistemic readings within the same plane. The existence of SAC-1 and SAC-2 suggests a continuity between content and epistemic readings. We can express causation with various perspective structures; typical content, epistemic and speech act sentences are just a part of these.

Next, I attempted to confront the continuity between content and epistemic readings. Some examples of *kara* sentences cannot be categorized in either content or epistemic readings; they seem to have features of both readings. I argued that those sentences (static causals) express particular realizations of association made by the speaker. Even though they express events in the world, like content readings, the knowledge of the speakers is implied and the sentences resemble epistemic readings. On the other hand, typical causals (dynamic causals) are based on causal laws. A causal law and association are very different in the sense that the former belongs to the world and the latter belongs to the knowledge of the speaker. However, they are both based on contingency. A causal law has to be based on a perfect contingency. Association can be contingent to various degrees. Imperfect contingency suggests the existence of the speaker who makes the association. That is, the speaker's state of mind (intentionality) is displayed. In contrast, when the contingency is perfect, it is regarded as a part of the world structure. In this sense, static causals exhibit a higher involvement of the speaker than dynamic causals.

The notion of 'subject involvement' integrates two analyses. Content (including SAC), epistemic, and speech act readings can be ordered on the first speaker involvement scale, which measures the speaker's involvement in reporting causal relations. The involvement of the speaker is higher when the speaker's perspective is more necessary in reporting causation. The second speaker involvement scale measures the speaker's involvement in constructing the reported relationship. Static causals that display the speaker's intentionality have high speaker involvement in this scale. We were able to see the continuity between content and epistemic readings, and how all the other readings are related, by using these two scales.

The scales show two different ways to use perspectives. The speaker involvement in the first scale affects the detection of perspectives, and thus the clause linkage. The degree of speaker involvement is part of the conveyed information. On the other hand, high speaker involvement in the second scale can invite the sharing of perspectives or the sharing of intentionality. The sentence may not be informative, but it affects interaction.

6.2 Grammar from a first-person point of view

Sweetser's (1990) widely accepted analysis of complex sentences is based on force dynamics. That is, in cognitive linguistics, the analysis of complex sentences is based on the categorization of the described relations. The analysis in this book has shown that there are examples of complex sentences (such as SAC and static causals) that can only be analyzed by paying attention to the speaker's involvement in describing a relationship.

To analyze grammar by paying attention to the speaker involvement is to view the grammar from a first-person point of view. Grammar reflects how the speaker sees the world. The speaker's perspective is given in the sentences. On the other hand, grammar based on force dynamics is a description of grammar from the third person's point of view. The description of grammatical structure is not biased by any kind of perspective. It focuses on what is described.[45]

Naturally, analysis from a third-person point of view analyzes the description of the outer world very well. Emphasis must be placed on the fact that the speaker's inner state can be analyzed from a third-person point of view.[46] As Sweetser's analysis of epistemic domains shows, expressions that are originally used to express relations in the objective world are often used to express the pure inner state of the speaker: that is, there is a metaphorical extension from the content domain to the epistemic domain. The problem occurs when a relation is a mixture of subjective expression and objective description; this is difficult to analyze from a third-person point of view, as it is difficult to separate how the speaker feels from what the speaker is trying to describe. I call expressions that describe a mixture of the subjective and objective states the expression of an 'interface' between the inner and outer state of the speaker. Grammar in the first person point of view provides an advantage in analyzing the expressions of interface. The usages of causals, such as SAC or static causals, that were pointed out in this book are also expressions of an interface. These expressions are based on a dynamic interaction between the objective and subjective axes (in the sense of Langacker 1991b).

Cognitive linguistics attempts to ground grammar in cognition. Representative studies, such as those by Langacker (1991a) and Talmy (2000), propose a form of analyzing sentences that is based on a 'force-dynamic relationship' (Talmy, 1988) or movement. A transmission of energy is a relationship that can be observed stably from a third-person point of view.

While there is no holistic analysis of sentences from a first-person perspective in cognitive linguistics, there is in traditional Japanese linguistics. Kawabata's analysis (1985, 2004) is strongly influenced by phenomenology. He contends that simple sentences reflect the structure of judgments (the processes of understanding something). Simple sentences are dyadic: they have subjects and predicates because judgments can be broken down into what has to be understood and the process of understanding. Kawabata argues that among all types of sentences, a static sentence with an adjectival predicate reflects the structure of judgment most closely. In contrast, typical sentences in the analyses by Langacker (1991a) and Talmy (2000) are dynamic sentences with verb predicates. In Kawabata's analysis, a simple sentence expresses the speaker's sanctioning of an event. I assume that complex sentences express a speaker's sanctioning of the relation between the events.

Table 6.1 Grammatical theories from the first- and third-person points of view

	Third-person point of view	*First-person point of view*
Simple sentence	Description of the force dynamics in an event (Talmy, 2000)	Expression of the speaker's sanctioning of an event (Kawabata, 1985)
Complex sentence	Description of the force dynamics between two events (Sweetser, 1990)	Expression of the speaker's sanctioning of the relation between the events (*This book*)

I am not trying to say that we have to discard conventional analysis from the third person point of view, since it is powerful in giving an integrated explanation for major examples. As pointed out by Langacker (2005), even when an analysis from the third-person point of view is useful, a first-person point of view (that is, how the speaker sees the relationship) underlies the grammar. In the analysis from the third-person point of view, the categories tend to be discrete; in the analysis from the first-person point of view, the categories tend to be continuous.

6.3 Contributions to and from other areas of cognitive science

Through the analysis of *kara* sentences, I explored the possibility of constructing grammar from a first-person point of view. To explore such a possibility in the framework of cognitive linguistics is to find a new way to ground grammar in cognition.

I am especially going to focus on studies in two fields that share the view presented in this book. Developmental psychology offers many candidates for a cognitive ground into which we may ground language. Artificial life lets us inquire into the dynamism that connects those cognitive grounds and grammar. It is an effective approach to discover whether our hypothesis is adequate or not, since we can test the emergence and development of grammar in artificial life but not in linguistics. Below, I will introduce works in these two fields that relate to the analysis of *kara* in this book.

First of all, observations in developmental psychology, especially research on autistic children, seem to offer a lot of supporting evidence for the work in this book. Autistic children have difficulties with perspective detection (Baron-Cohen 1995; Loveland & Tunali, 1993), perception of imperfect contingency (Gergely & Watson, 1999; Koós & Gergely, 2001), proto-declarative communication such as participatory joint attention (Gómez, Sarria, & Tamarit 1993; Mundy, Sigman & Kasari, 1993) and imitating the manner of motion (Hobson, 2002; Nadel, 2002). Autistic children are also known for atypical usages of language (Tager-Flusberg, 1993, 2000). Grammatical analysis from the first-person point of view might give a clue to the relationship between the linguistic and cognitive anomalies of autistic children.

To use a grammar from the first-person point of view, the speaker needs to understand how others see the world. That is, he or she needs to understand the perspective of others. This is not the case in using a grammar from a third-person point of view. Autistic children are known to lack the theory of mind, which is an ability to understand others' minds (cf. Section 5.4.2). Therefore, it is natural that the topics which are discussed in studying autistic syndrome are related with the study in this book. That is, both topics involve the relationship between speaker (subject) involvement and grammar (rule).

Second, let's take a look at studies which construct artificial agents to understand the nature of life (which is an area called artificial life or A-life; cf. Elman, 1998). These may be robots or computationally simulated agents. The embodied nature of cognition is one of the phenomena that many researchers in A-life try to construct and understand. Agents are assigned a sensori-motor system (that is, embodied) to interact with the environment. What emerges and how it emerges through interaction is then observed. For example, deictic expression emerges in Steels's model (2005) through linguistic interaction. Ikegami and Iizuka (2003) observe the emergence of intersubjectivity by being sensitive to the imperfect contingency of others. In Morimoto and Ikegami (2004), dynamical categorization (which results in the radial category) emerges through the interaction between the agent and the shapes (As we have discussed in Section 4.5; also found in Iizuka & Ikegami, 2004; Marocco & Floreano, 2002; Scheier & Pfeifer, 1995; Tani & Nolfi, 1998). There have also been attempts to determine how agents make distinctions between themselves and the environment (Ikegami, 2000, 2004). Finally, based on the hypothesis that I proposed in the previous chapter, we carried out a simulation to observe the emergence of instrumental and participatory joint attention, which can lead to the emergence of types of sentences (Uno, Marocco, Ikegami & Nolfi, 2008).

Not only by analyzing language, but also by trying to construct language, A-life aims to understand what language is. There is a newly occurring trend toward collaborative research between A-life and linguistics and other areas of cognitive science. This area is called 'evolutionary linguistics.'

The following table shows that an analysis from a first-person point of view can bridge cognitive linguistics and other areas of cognitive science.

Table 6.2   Related works in other fields

Key concepts in each chapter	Related works	
	Developmental psychology	Artificial life
Ch.2 Detecting perspectives	Baron-Cohen (1995), Loveland and Tunali (1993)	Steels (2005)
Ch.3 A trend towards imperfect contingency	Gergely and Watson (1999), Koós and Gergely (2001)	Ikegami and Iizuka (2003)
Ch.4 Interaction between the speaker and the events in the categorization	Hobson (2002), Nadel (2002)	Morimoto and Ikegami (2004), Scheier and Pfeifer (1995), etc.
Ch.5 Sharing perspectives or participatory joint attention	Mundy, Sigman, and Kasari (1993), Gómez, Sarria, and Tamarit (1993)	Steels (2003), Uno, Marocco, Nolfi, and Ikegami (2008)

I believe that linguistics, including the analysis of *kara* in this book, can contribute to cognitive science by analyzing the form of cognition that characterizes language.

Notes

1. In Japanese, the subordinate clause usually precedes the main clause. Compared to English, the clausal order is restricted. Connectives appear at the end of the subordinate clauses. They are attached to the predicates in the subordinate clauses.
2. Interestingly, some relations can be expressed with both connectives almost equally, as follows (Nagano, 1988: 72):

    (a) *koko   wa   umi ga   tikai   (   ) kaze ga   suzusii.*
    here   TOP   sea   NOM be.close   because wind NOM   be.cool
    'The wind is cool because the sea is nearby.'

    For this example, 15.7% chose kara and 23.0 % chose node. I will come back to this example in Section 4.3.5.

3. Takubo argued that the former *kara* expresses 'reasons of action' and the latter *kara* expresses 'grounds of judgment.'
4. Iwasaki (1995), based on Takubo (1987), has renamed these two types of *kara*. The first one is called 'the cause/reason of events' because it modifies the propositional level. The latter modifies the modality level, so he called it 'the grounds of modal attitudes.'
5. Masuoka (1997) points out that there are differences between *kara* and *node* which cannot be explained by the difference between Types B and C.
6. The form of the verb in complex sentences is known to indicate the syntactic linkage between the clauses. Thus, the relationship between the form and the meaning of clausal linkage is indicated in this study.
7. Takubo (1992: 55) explains mental spaces as follows: 'A domain with internal structures connected to each other is called a mental space. Mental space is defined as an incremental set and is structured with elements. It is established in the discourse and while the discourse proceeds it changes. This level is not truth conditional but since it provides patterns of inference about the world or action, it connects reality and linguistic expression. That is, it works as a cognitive interface which connects language and the world outside'.

8   Sweetser (1996) points out that Fillmore's argument that epistemic stances towards the protasis and the apodosis have to be the same, and Fauconnier's analysis that in conditionals the protasis is completely embedded in the mental space built by the apodosis, are saying the same thing. Here are the examples from Sweetser (1996, 329-330).

   (a) *If he'll be better tomorrow, he'll go to the show.
   (b) If it'll rain tomorrow, then we'll bring our umbrellas.
   (c) If you will be going to Paris, why did you buy a ticket to Tokyo?

   Usually, "will" cannot be used inside the conditional clause except when it expresses intention. This explains why (a) is ungrammatical. In the case of the epistemic reading in (b) and the speech act reading in (c), this restriction is eased, so they escape from being grammatically incorrect. Sweetser explains that (b) and (c), which have non-content readings, have a different embedding of mental spaces. Cutrer (1994) has a different opinion. It is argued that the difference between the three readings has to do with their different structures of mental spaces. Cutrer also argues that all types of conditionals have the same structure of spaces, and that their only difference is that in content conditionals the protasis may be either prediction or fact, but in epistemic conditionals it has to be fact.

9   It is possible to read (3) as 'Yoko bought a toy because her child was going to cry.' In this case, this sentence would be categorized as an ordinary content reading sentence. However, I am going to deal with the sentence as translated.

10 This point is disputed. While IRH regards cosubordination as a tighter juncture than subordination, others (e.g., Ohori, 2000) suggest that it is the other way around.

11 Some content words assume perspectives—for example, adjectives that express judgment or nouns that express direction; however, these content words are more biased towards the speaker. For example, *azayakana* 'splendid' in the following sentence cannot be used when the speaker thinks that it is not splendid, but the protagonist thinks that it is.

   (a) azayakana   syoori   o   <u>osame-ta</u>$_{\text{P-D}}$ kara   Taroo   wa   <u>siawaseda</u> $_{\text{P-M}}$.
       splendid   victory   ACC   score-PAST   because   Taroo   TOP be. happy
       'Taroo is happy because he scored a splendid victory.'

12 Here is an example of the contrast between content and epistemic readings. When the event of the dependent clause follows the event of the main clause and precedes the speech time, in content reading the dependent clause takes past tense as shown in (a), while in epistemic reading the causal clause takes non-past tense, as shown in (b).

(a) Content reading

Mori-san	*wa*	*Pekin*	*e*	*iku* $_{P\text{-}D}$	*kara*	*tyuugokugo*	*no*
Mr. Mori	TOP	Beijing	LOC	go	because	Chinese	GEN

kenkyukai	*ni*	*sannka*	*si-ta* $_{P\text{-}M}$.
research.meeting	LOC	participate-PAST	

'Mr. Mori's trip to Beijing is the reason for his participation in the Chinese linguistics meeting.'

(b) Epistemic reading

Pekin	*e*	*it-ta* $_{P\text{-}D}$	*kara*	*Mori-san*	*wa*	*tyuugokugo*	*no*
Beijing	LOC	go-PAST	because	Mr.Mori	TOP	Chinese	GEN

kenkyuukai	*ni*	*sanka*	*si-ta* $_{P\text{-}M}$.
esearch meeting	LOC	participate-PAST	

'Because of (my knowledge of) Mr. Mori's trip to Beijing (I conclude that) he participated in the Chinese linguistics meeting.'

13 The result I am going to show in this section is consistent with what we have seen in the previous section. It is worth noting that the examples of content readings that will be used are very rare. However, I performed the analysis since it is required by the framework.

14 If the sentence expresses a causal relationship between events and not actions, there is no readily conceivable separation between A (E-M) and D (E-M). In this case, only the positions for D (E-M) work as an E-M.

15 We saw in 3.1.2 that when a distinction can be made between a decision to act (D (E-M)) and the act itself (A (E-D)), the perspective of the dependent clause is located at the time when the protagonist made the decision. This indicates that the perspective resides in the mental state of the protagonist in a content reading.

16 Fujii (2000) points out that when the form *mono-da-kara* is used instead of *kara*, there is an implication of the negative evaluation of the event in the dependent clause by the subject of the main clause.

17 In the Discourse Representation Theory (DRT) of Kamp and Rohrer (1983), the tense marker is regarded as an indicator of the reference points.

18 At the clausal level, the next target is the conditionals. Conditionals are discussed in the framework of mental spaces. Perspectives can explain which semantic level is related to syntax, including the linkage. This analysis treats the linkage type, such as cosubordination and backshift, equally. In addition, Dancygier (1998: 149) notes that the default clause order of *because* sentences is q–p, while that of *if* sentences is p–q. This corre-

sponds with the hierarchy of mental spaces.

19 I recognize the importance of subjective construal, which sustains causal laws (Fauconnier & Turner, 2002; Lakoff & Johnson, 1999), but this is a different issue from causal relationships. Even if the creation of causal laws is subjective, I contend that it belongs to the external world. I will come back to this problem in Section 3.5.1.

20 The denotative relation between 'tree' on the one hand and 'oak' or 'beech' on the other is also an example of subsumption. 'Oak' and 'beech' are subsumed under the category 'tree'.

21 The association between 'white things' and 'snow' is natural in Japanese but very tenuous in English.

22 In this book, I use the term 'causation' to refer only to the realization of a causal law.

23 As Seto (1997) points out, in Langacker's (1987) theory of semantic extension, the 'adjacency of things' and the 'subsuming of categories' are the two most important features. My analysis is the first step towards revealing the connection between these two relations.

24 In this book, when a sentence can be exchanged with another sentence, and this change does not affect the flow of the text, I will say, 'the meaning does not change markedly.'

25 Following Sweetser (1990), this categorization is used in Dancygier and Sweetser (2000), Maat and Degand (2001) and Sweetser and Dancygier (2005). Its application to Japanese complex sentences has been investigated by Ohori (2000) and Fujii (2001).

26 I extracted the examples marked 'CSJ' from *The Corpus of Spontaneous Japanese* by Japan's priority-area research project, known as Spontaneous Speech: Corpus and Processing Technology.

27 The causal laws and connotative relationships given here are just examples.

28 Just as Sweetser (1990) did, I am arguing for the advantages of the specific reading of the examples. Each sentence may itself have several interpretations. The interpretation is specified in brackets after each example.

29 The rhetorical relation that Sato (1987) referred to as 'reverse-metaphor' is also based on this relationship (i.e. a connotative relation with prejudice). For example, *kyoo-onna* ('a lady from Kyoto') or *aitu wa seizika da kara* ('because he is a politician'). Sato explains that in the case of reverse metaphors, meaning changes when there is no overlap between the connotations, although there is an overlap between the denotations.

30 In a different context, the sentences in (16) and (17) can be used as explanations for why the speaker feels lonely, or why the speaker thinks that she is shy. In this case, the sentences are examples of dynamic *kara* sentences with content reading.

31 In English, too, there are causals that appear to express static relations. An example is the

following lyric by the pop group, The Beatles: "Because the sky is blue it makes me cry." Inquiries of several native speakers suggest that English prefers to express in two sentences or by juxtaposition the static relations that in Japanese are expressed in complex sentences. This is consistent with my analysis in this chapter.

32 It is known in the theory of mind that to infer the minds of others requires a cognitive ability that differs from that used in the discovery of physical causation (Baron-Cohen, 1995). See Section 5.4.2 for related discussion.

33 As noted in Chapter 2, since it is not possible to apply tests to discover the perspective of non-volitional causals, the tests were carried out for volitional content causals.

34 Static causals are based on the relationship between a notion and its feature (connotative relation). This is a special type of association in general. I use the term association in chapter 4, 5 and 6 to characterize static causals because it is conceptually easier and the type of association is not important in these chapters.

35 Here, I want to point out the similarity between SAC-1 and static *kara* sentences. In SAC-1, the protagonist's involvement brings about a cause-effect relationship. For the protagonist, the cause and the effect lose directionality. On the other hand, in static and epistemic content, the speaker's involvement relates the two events or situations. One of the interesting findings in this book is that while causation is strongly characterized with directionality, *kara* sentences, which typically express causation, can be used to express paratactic relations in various ways.

36 Iwasaki's (1994) analysis of SAC-1, introduced in Section 2.3.1.2, includes both *node* and *kara*.

37 See Section 3.5 for an explanation of *mono* in Japanese.

38 Some studies in developmental psychology imply that there is a connection between the cognition of 'how,' the detection of perspectives, and linguistic structure. For example, autistic children cannot use language naturally, especially when the perspective is related (Tager-Flusberg, 2000). They can imitate what others are doing but not how others are doing it (Hobson, 2002; see also Nadel, 2002). The relationship between the expression of 'how' and language is also argued in Kita (1997), Kita and Özyürek (2003), Tomasello (2003) and Slobin (2004).

39 The redundant nature of static causals can also be observed in other respects. For example, sentence (1) can be replaced with (a) or (b), in most contexts.

(a) *aki   da   ne.*
    autumn   COP   FP

(b) *simizimisuru   ne.*
       feel.lonely   FP
40 In old Japanese, imperatives were also expressed in a construction similar to a one-word sentence.
41 I also categorize Honda's (2003) examples of joint attention as the ground-dependent type. They express the movement of the speaker towards the object or the relationship. The examples in (b) and (c) are used for instrumental JA. The example in (a) can be used for participatory JA.
   (a) Phenomenal description of events
       ame   ga   *hut-teiru.*
       rain   NOM   fall-ASP
       'It is raining.'
   (b) Particle-less argument construction
       hasami   aru?
       scissors   have
       'Do you have any scissors?'
   (c) Left dislocation
       mimi   kyappu   are   hazusi-te.
       ear   cap   that   take.off (IMP)
       'Earmuffs, take them off.'
42 The computer program ELIZA, created by Joseph Weizenbaum, is another example of ground-independent participatory JA. This program makes people feel sympathetic towards ELIZA, which just repeats what people have said to it, with a little modification; that is, participatory JA is established through the use of redundant replies.
   (a) Person: *I have a headache.*
       ELIZA: *You have a headache?*
43 Lyons (1977) focused on the relationship between speech act theory (Austin, 1962; Searle, 1969) and grammar. In the future, I intend to elaborate on Lyons's analysis of sentence types, based on my observations in this study and grammatical theories in traditional Japanese linguistics.
44 We have started to explore the emergence of the prototype of exclamative and declarative sentences in computer simulation based on the discussion in this chapter (Uno, Marocco, Nolfi, & Ikegami, 2008).
45 Honda (2004, 2005) and Gärdenfors (2008) also emphasize the importance of the first person view of grammar.

46 Recently, there are more studies in cognitive linguistics that focus on the interaction between subjective and objective perspectives (e.g., Sweetser & Ferrari, 2007; Verhargen, 2005). Some recent analyses of conditionals reflect this trend (e.g., Dancygier, 2007; Sweetser, 2007). These studies assume a clear distinction between subjective and objective domains, and attempt to observe the interaction between these domains, while the study in this book tries to analyze the inseparability of subjectivity and objectivity in some linguistic phenomena.

日本語の読者のための内容紹介

視点の追跡と共有

—理由の接続助詞「から」を含む複文の認知言語学的分析—

はじめに

　認知言語学は、言語の認知的基盤を追及するアプローチです。特に、言葉と「人々が物事をどうみるか」の関係について多くの成果を出してきました。

　認知言語学が生まれる少し前、英語学者のReddy（1979）は英語で用いられる「言葉についての言葉」を分析し、それが英語話者の言語観に与える影響について考え、論じました。Reddyが注目したのは以下のような表現です。

- You have to put each concept into words very carefully.
  （十分に注意して考えを言葉の中に入れなさい。）
- The sentence was filled with emotion.
  （文には感情が満ちていた。）
- I don't get any feelings of anger out of his words.
  （彼の言葉からどんな怒りも取り出すことはできなかった。）

　これらの文は、一つのイメージに基づいています。話し手は言葉に考えや思いを入れて、言葉を受け取った聞き手はそこから考えや思いをとり出す、というイメージです。言葉は話し手と聞き手をつなぐ管のようなものです。Reddyは英語を支配しているこのような言葉に対するイメージを「導管メタファー（コンジット）」と名付けました。

　英語を使うことで導管メタファーに慣れてしまうと、言葉で自分の思いが寸分違わず相手に伝わるのだ、と思い込みがちです。このことを憂いたReddyは、導管メタファーに縛られている英語話者の有り様を、意地悪な魔法使いによって記憶を一部奪われている状態に喩えました。本当は思いや気持をそのまま誰かに渡すことなどできるはずがありません。話し手はなんとかして気持

を正確に言葉に置き換えようとし、聞き手は一生懸命に言葉を手がかりに話し手の思いを復元しようとします。そんな中でコミュニケーションが成功するのは大変稀なことです。ところが、その置き換えや復元の作業に関する記憶が奪われてしまったとしましょう。人々は思いを直に受け渡しているのだと思うようになり、コミュニケーションがうまくいかないことに苛立ち始めるのです。

その後、認知言語学の先駆けとして Lakoff と Johnson の本（1980）が世に出ました。この本は Reddy の議論を発展させ、言葉についての言葉が導管メタファーに基づいているように、他の多くの事柄についての言葉も様々なメタファーに基づいているのだ、と論じました。つまり、言葉を使って何かを述べることはある種の記憶喪失になることに他ならないのです。中でも、言葉について言葉で語ることは、記憶を失ったまま、その記憶を奪った魔法について述べるような難しいことです。Reddy はその困難に挑戦したのです。

さて、言葉、あるいは魔法使いが意地悪だったかどうかはともかくとして、Reddy や Lakoff と Johnson そして、それに続く認知言語学の研究者達は、言葉と人の物事の見方とが深く関わっていることを示してきました。その一例がメタファーです。そしてその更に具体的な一例として導管メタファーがあるのです。

本書も、カラ文がどのような見方、つまり視点の取り方、と関わっているのか、ということから始めて、その見方の揺らぎ、そしてその揺らぎの拡大について論じます。カラ文を通じて本書が扱う「見方」の問題はメタファーではなく、ある見方があったとしてそれはどこからの誰にとっての見方なのか（ダイクシス）と自分の見方を他人と共有するメカニズム（ジョイント・アテンション）に関わります。

いくつもの先行研究や現在進行中の研究に支えられて、本書は存在しています。複文の意味と形の関係を探究した研究（大堀、2000 など）や条件表現から人間の推論について考察した研究（坂原、1985 など）を発展させようとして、ここに辿りつきました。研究する中で、認知言語学が「見方」を扱ってきた経緯と意義（西村、2008 など）を、そして、そのような「見方」の研究の向こう側（本多、2006 など）を考えざるを得ませんでした。結果として、言語学以外の多くの分野と一緒に新しい言語研究の形を作り上げていくことが必要だ、と思うに至りました。それが、分析的な研究手法を用いる言語学を補うような、構成論的アプローチをとる複雑系の科学（池上、2007 など）に取り組むきっかけとなりました。言葉を切り刻んで調べるのではなくて、言葉が自らについて告白しはじめるのを待つ、そのような研究の方略を考えていく、その始まりが、カラ文の分析の中にありました。

文献

Lakoff, George & Mark Johnson. 1980. *Metaphors We Live By*. Chicago: University of Chicago Press.

Reddy, Michael.J. 1979. "The conduit metaphor: A case of frame conflict in our language about language" Andrew Ortony ed. *Metaphor and Thought*. Cambridge: Cambridge University Press, 284-297.

池上高志．2007．『動きが生命をつくる』青土社

大堀壽夫．2000．「言語的知識としての構文―複文の類型論に向けて」坂原茂（編）『認知言語学の発展』ひつじ書房，281-316.

坂原茂．1985．『日常言語の推論』東京大学出版会

西村義樹．2008．「換喩の認知言語学」森雄一・西村義樹・山田進・米山三明（編）『ことばのダイナミズム』くろしお出版，71-88.

本多啓．2006．「認知意味論、コミュニケーション、共同注意―捉え方（理解）の意味論から見せ方（提示）の意味論へ―」『語用論研究』8, 1-13.

本書の構成

第一章：イントロダクション

1-1 目的

　本書は理由の接続助詞「から」を含む複文（カラ文）の意味の広がりを認知言語学的に分析する。カラ文は理由文の一種である。理由文とは、例えば英語の *because* などの理由の接続語を含む複文で、典型的には因果関係を表す。

　本研究は、カラ文を話者の視点との関わりで分析することで、日本語学や認知言語学でのこれまでの研究を発展させて、カラ文の意味と形の関係や、意味拡張についてこれまで以上に明らかにすることを目指した。更にもう一つ、目指したことがある。話者は言語を用いて、「私」の心の中で起きていることも、また「私」の外で起きていることも同じように表す。カラ文の分析を通じて、この点から言語を見直そうと試みた。「私」の外と内という異なる二つの領域の認識を言語はどのようにつないでいるのかを探ることは言語学だけではなく、広く人間の認知の解明にとって重要である。

　では、どうして言葉と「私」の問題を考えるために、特別にカラ文を扱うのか。それは、カラ文など一部の理由文は、他の複文に比べても特にはっきりと、物理的因果関係と話者の内面の因果関係の両方を表すからである。例文

(1) は話者の外部で起きていることを表し、(2) は話者の内部の推論関係を表している。

 (1) 大風が吹いたから木が倒れた。
 (2) 明かりがついているからお隣さんはもう帰宅した。

　先行研究を踏まえ、(1) と (2) のような例文の関係を考察するところから本書の研究は始まる。どうして、話者は「私」の外部の因果関係と内部の因果関係を、同じカラ文を用いて表すことができるのか、に注目する。それは、話し手の文成立への関与を見ることにつながる。分析していく中で、カラ文成立には二種類の話者関与が考えられる、と指摘した。
　一つ目は、カラ文の表す関係の報告への話者関与である。二つ目はカラ文の表す関係そのものへ話者関与である。話し手の視点は、前者では聞き手にとって因果関係を理解するために「追跡」されるべきものであり、後者では、聞き手にとって共有されるべきものとなる。

1-2 先行研究

　永野（1952）は理由の接続助詞ノデとカラの使い分けについて初めて本格的に論じ、ノデは客観的関係を、カラは主観的関係を表すとした。その後、田窪（1987）は、永野の指摘した二種類の関係は接続助詞の違いというより、因果関係の二種であるとし、どちらもカラで表されると指摘した。上で見た(1) は客観的関係を表すカラの、(2) は主観的関係を表すカラの例となる。ここから、二種類のカラの関係が問われることになる。
　田窪はこの二種のカラの違いを統語的な観点から捉え、カラ節の主節への従属度の違いであるとした。田窪は、南（1974, 1993）の分類法に基づき、客観的な関係を表すカラ節は述語に時制までは含めることができるが、認識的モダリティを含むことができないタイプ（B類）であり、主観的な関係を表すカラ節は述語に時制はもちろんのこと、認識的モダリティを含むことができるタイプ（C類）であると指摘した。
　それでは、意味的にはどのような二種類なのか。この問いへの答えは、認知言語学者 Sweetser（1990）による理由の接続語の研究にみられる。（田窪のカラ文の研究と Sweetser の理由の接続語の研究の対応については Higashiizumi [2006] など。）Sweetser は推論関係や発話行為が物理世界（実質的領域）に見立てられることがしばしばある、と論じた。（このような見立てはメタファーと呼ばれ、Lakoff and Johnson [1980] で詳しく分析されている。）そして本来は実質的領域に属する、力の働きかけの関係（フォース・ダイナミクス）が認

識的領域に属する推論関係にあてはめられたのが（2）のような「認識的読み」と呼ばれる理由の接続語の解釈であるとする。（1）の理由の接続語カラの解釈は「実質的読み」と呼ばれる。更に（3）のように発話を可能にするものと発話行為の間に力の働きかけの関係があてはめられることがあり、その場合のカラの解釈は「発話行為的読み」と呼ばれる。

(3) うるさいから静かにしなさい。

さて、そもそも永野が論じたのは、話者がどのように因果関係を結ぶか、であった。この論点はノデとカラの違いや二種類のカラを説明しようとする長い論争の過程で失われてしまった。本書では、永野より後の日本語学そして認知言語学の研究の発展を踏まえつつ、新しいコンテクストでもう一度話者とカラ文の関係を追及する。

1-3 概要

本書では（1）と（2）（3）（とりわけ（1）と（2））をつなぐのはどのような認知のあり方か、を問うことからはじめる。

第二章では田窪やSweetserなどの既存の研究を応用することで、第三章ではそれとは異なる方法で実質的読みと認識的読みの関係を探る。第四章では二つの研究方法を、カラ文への話者関与という観点から統合する。結果、先行研究では見られなかったようなカラ文の意味の広がりを示すことができる。第五章では、残された問題を解決するため、相互作用の中でのカラ文の働きを見る。そして第六章ではまとめと展望を述べる。

以下、この和文の内容紹介では、例文番号の横に本書でのカラ文の分類名を挙げるが、スペースの関係で、説明に先行して分類名が登場する箇所もある。

第二章：意味と形をつなぐ視点構造

> 私がちぎったバゲットを、彼が、その手ずから食べました。彼が咀嚼を始めると、実際にはしっかりと、口の中で小麦の甘みが広がっていましたが、これまで彼が食べ慣れていたパンの味と、「コティディアン」のそれはあまりに違うため、というより、彼がパンの味と思っていたもののうち、このパンからはやってこないものがあったので、そのことの違和感というか、物足りなさの方が、彼にとっての前面にやってきてしまっていて、小麦の甘みにまで意識が届いていませんでした。バゲットのカリカリした表面についている、白い細かい粉が、部屋の床に舞い落ちました。その粒子を浮き上がらせる

ような光が、そのとき、部屋の中に差していたわけではなかったため、私や彼は、それを見ませんでした。

(岡田利規「楽観的な方のケース」)

　誰の視点から語るか、にまつわるルール。それは、文章のレベルにも、文のレベルにも、そして、文より小さな節のレベルにも存在します。そのルールに巧みに挑むことで、上に引用した文章は、語っている視点があるはずの場所をどこかへと、鮮やかに解き放ってしまいました。
　第二章ではカラの含まれる節で描かれる事態、つまり原因や理由が、誰の視点から描かれているかのルールを考えます。それを手がかりに、実質的読みと認識的読みの意味や形の違いについて説明することを試みます。

2-1 カラ文と視点
　カラ文の実質的読みと認識的読みの関係を探ろうとしたとき、先行研究から得られた最大の手掛かりは、二つの読みとカラ節の主節への従属度との関わりである（本和文内容紹介1-2参照）。従属度は従属節の中にどのような助動詞が現れるかによって測ることができる（南1993）。カラ文の二つの読みと関連して問題となる助動詞は、時制を表すもの（「た」）と認識的モダリティを表すもの（「だろう」「らしい」など）である。ここでは、この二種類の助動詞はどちらも、視点を示す（ダイクティックな表現である）という共通点があることに注目する。例えば、「た」が過去を表す時には、いつの時点から見ての過去なのかという基準点がある。「だろう」の場合は推論を行っている誰かの観点がある。

2-2 視点構造を用いた分析
　本章では、カラ文の実質的読みと認識的読みの違いを知るために、カラ節で表わされる事態を描く視点について、カラ節の時制や認識的モダリティの解釈から探った。
　第一に、カラ節の時制や認識的モダリティの分析から、通常の実質的読みの場合にはカラ節事態を描く視点は主節事態あるいは主節主語にあり、認識的読みの場合には発話の場あるいは話し手に視点がある、という傾向を指摘する。以下で具体的な例を見てみよう。

　　(4) 通常の実質的読み
　　　　森さんは北京へ行くから中国語の研究会に参加した。

［解釈：森さんには当時北京へ行く予定があったことが原因で森さんは中国語の研究会に参加した。］
　(5) 認識的読み
　　　森さんは北京へ行ったから中国語の研究会に参加した（だろう）。
　　　［解釈：「森さんには当時北京に行く予定が当時あった」という私の知識から「森さんは中国語の研究会に参加した」と私は判断する。］

　どちらの文でも、発話の時点に対しての出来事の生起の順序は同じである。最初に森さんが中国語の研究会に参加し（主節事態）、次に森さんが北京へ行き（カラ節事態）、そしてこれらの文が発話される（発話事態）のはその更に後である。

　実質的読みである例文（4）では、カラ節の述語は非過去（「行く」）となっている。カラ節の時制解釈は主節の時制を基準としているといえる。一方で、認識的読みの例である（5）ではカラ節の述語は過去（「行った」）となっている。カラ節の時制解釈は発話時を基準とし、主節の時制に対して独立であるといえる。それぞれのカラ節の時制解釈を「主節依存」タイプ、「独立」タイプと呼ぶ。

　第二に、カラ節の時制の解釈にはもう一つのタイプがあるという問題を考える。それが次の（7）の例に見られる。通常の実質的読みである（6）と比べてみよう。

　(6) 通常の実質的読み
　　　子供が泣いたからよう子はおもちゃを買った。
　　　［解釈：子供が泣いたことが原因でよう子はおもちゃを買った。］
　(7) SAC-1（特殊な実質的読み）
　　　子供が泣くからよう子はおもちゃを買った。
　　　［解釈：子供が泣いたことが原因でよう子はおもちゃを買った。］

　再び、どちらの文でも、発話の時点に対しての出来事の生起の順序は同じである。まず、子どもが泣き（カラ節事態）、よう子がおもちゃを買い（主節事態）、その後にこれらの文は発話されている（発話事態）。

　(6)は通常の実質的読みであり、(4)と同様にカラ節の時制解釈は主節依存である。ところが、(7)の文では、(6)と同じ事態間の因果関係を表しているのに、(6)とは異なりカラ節の述語に「た」が現れない。本書では、Van Valin (2005) 他の複文の類型論的な分析から、(7)のような文ではカラ節における時制の表示が抑止されており、その代りに主節述語で表わされた時制

が、カラ節と主節の間で共有されているのだ、と考える。このようなカラ節の時制の解釈を「抑止」タイプと呼ぶことにする。抑止タイプには (8) のような例もある。

　　(8) SAC-2 (特殊な実質的読み)
　　　　飛び出すから彼は怪我をした。

　問題は、表されている事態間の関係だけを見れば、(7) と (8) は実質的読みに分類されるのにも関わらず、(4) や (6) のような通常の実質的読みとは異なる時制の解釈を持つということである。実質的読みはカラ節事態が主節依存、認識的読みはカラ節事態が主節から独立、という観察だけでは関係する全てのカラ文を説明できないのである。
　この問題の解決のために、本書ではカラ文の分析にあたって、視点だけではなく、「視点構造」を考えることにした。本書で視点構造と呼ぶのは、視点とそれに関係するメンタル・スペース (Fauconnier, 1985) の配置である。言いかえると、視点構造を考えるとは、単に事態を描写する基準点としての視点の位置を観察するだけではなく、以下の点も考慮に入れるということである。まず、発話事態、カラ節事態、主節事態などがどのように話者の心の中で関係付けられているか。次に、それらの事態に対して、話者や主節主語などの視点などはどう位置付けられるか。そして、以上の要素は発話の推移に伴ってどのように、配置を変えるか。
　Fauconnier は時制や認識的モダリティを表す表現が視点構造を示唆すると指摘し、Cutrer (1994) はそのルールを体系化した。本書では、Cutrer のルールをカラ文の分析に応用する。そうすると、上記で見たカラ文の通常の実質的読みと認識的読みの違いは次のように説明される。通常の実質的読みではカラ節事態のメンタル・スペースは主節の事態のメンタル・スペース (主節主語の視点) からのみ直接アクセスすることが可能で、発話事態のメンタル・スペース (話者の視点) からは直接アクセスできない。一方で、認識的読みでは発話事態のメンタル・スペースからカラ節事態と主節事態のメンタル・スペースに直接アクセスできる。
　更に問題の (7) や (8) のような抑止タイプの特殊な実質的読みについては、メンタル・スペースや視点の配置は通常の実質的読みと同じであるが、カラ節事態へのアクセスが通常の実質的読みとは異なり特殊なのだ、と分析する。(7) については主節主語の視点からの、(8) については話者の視点からのカラ節事態へのアクセスが特殊であると論じる。特に (8) のタイプについては、実質的読みでありながらも、話者の視点からカラ節事態にアクセスして

いるという点から、認識的読みに近い面もあると指摘する。そして、(7)のタイプは「SAC-1」、(8)のタイプは「SAC-2」と呼ぶ。(SAC は Special Access to Cause から。)

(7)のようなカラ文については岩崎(1994)の優れた先行研究があるが、そこでも(7)のタイプのカラ文と、(4)や(5)そして(8)などのタイプのカラ文との関連は捉えられていない。本書では、視点構造を考えることで、カラ文に関して、主節依存、独立そして抑止の三タイプのカラ節の時制解釈と Sweetser (1990) の扱う実質的・認識的読みという分類の関係を説明できる、と論じた。そして、この分析手法により(4)から(8)までのカラ文の意味的側面を、同一の平面上で扱うことができると示した。第四章では本章の分析を話者とカラ文との関わりという観点から捉えなおす。

2-3 複文の意味と形をつなぐ視点構造

第二章の終わりでは、「主節依存」「抑止」「独立」というカラ節の時制解釈に対応する視点構造を持ったカラ文は、それぞれ従位接続、等従位接続、等位接続と呼ばれる統語論的接続のタイプに属することを示した。(この三種の接続のタイプについては Van Valin [2005] など。) これは、カラ文の意味(実質的読みと認識的読み)と形(接続のタイプ)のつながりを考える際に、視点構造というレベルを考える必要性を示したことになるが、この結果はカラ文だけではなく、複文一般の分析にとって意味を持つ。複文の意味と形の対応に関して、量的な関係(結びつきの強さ)による分析は進んでいるが、質的な関係(結びつきの種類)による分析はまだ十分とは言えない。視点構造に着目することによって、後者の分析を押し進めることができるのではないか、と本書は提案した。

第三章：カラ文によって表される静的関係と動的関係

> 意味の弾性ということばづかいの趣旨は、第一に、固形的な自己同一性を表象したくないためであった。そして第二に、それでも未練がましくある程度の自己同一性を考えたいからでもあった。要するに、調子に乗って意味の流動性などと言いたくないからである。意味は液体や気体ではない。不思議な分節性を、たしかにそなえているからである。
>
> 意味はしなやかに伸縮するけれど、すぐ原形にもどろうとする(その原形はメートル原器のように固形物ではないが、しかし、おぼろげに《予想される》存在である、あるいは、おぼろげにしか予想されない存在である)。伸縮が限度を越えると、意味はこわ

れてしまう…。

(佐藤信夫『意味の弾性』)

　前章ではカラ文について、接続のタイプという形の側面と、実質的読みや認識的読みなどの意味の側面とが、視点構造を介して結びつく様を見ました。しかし、前章で扱った全ての例において、カラ文という形と、因果関係という意味の結びつきは確固たるものでした。それは、多くのカラ文や理由文の研究でも同様です。第三章ではカラ文と結びつく意味がしなやかに伸縮する様子を追います。因果関係を成り立たせている「働きかけの力」が薄らぐにつれて現れてくるのは、カラ文を述べる「私」の心の在り方です。

3-1 フォース・ダイナミクスを表さない理由文

　前章では、実質的読みと認識的読みの関係を視点構造に着目して分析した。第三章では、実質的読みと認識的読みの両方の性質を持っているように見えながら、どちらにも分類されないカラ文の存在を指摘し、分析した。
　もう一度確認すると、Sweetser は力の働きかけの関係(フォース・ダイナミクス [Talmy, 1988]) の見立て (メタファー [Lakoff & Johnson, 1980]) によって理由の接続語が多彩な意味を表すことができると論じた。実質的読みの例である (9) では、ある出来事が別の出来事を引き起こすという社会・物理的な力の働きかけの関係そのものが表されている。それに対して認識的読みの例である (10) では推論のプロセスがこのような社会・物理的な力の働きかけの関係に見立てられているのだとする。

　(9) 実質的読み、動的理由文
　　　大風が吹いたから木が倒れた。
　(10) 認識的読み、動的理由文
　　　明かりがついているからお隣さんはもう帰宅した(だろう)。

　本書は、カラ文の中には、力の働きかけを見出しにくく、Sweetser で提案されているようなフォース・ダイナミクスに基づく理由文の分類にはあてはまらないものがある、と指摘する。そして、通常の理由文が因果法則に基づいているのに対して、ここで指摘するフォース・ダイナミクスを見出しにくいカラ文は連想関係に基づいていると分析した。以下で例を用いて説明する。
　次の (11) には少なくとも二つの解釈がある。

(11) 動的理由文、静的理由文
　　　秋だから葉が色づく。

　紅葉の仕組みを詳しく知っている場合や、そうでなくとも秋であることと葉の色の変化の間に何かしら因果連鎖があると意識して(11)の文を言ったり、聞いたりする場合、この文は(9)のような実質的領域のフォース・ダイナミクスを表す理由文である。一方、次のような解釈も可能である。話者又は聞き手は秋という季節にいろいろな側面を見出している。赤とんぼが飛んでいるという側面、しみじみと悲しい気持ちになるという側面などである。そのような側面の一つとして、秋には葉が色づく、と捉えている。この場合には、(11)の文にフォース・ダイナミクスを見出すことは難しくなる。秋とその一面としての紅葉、という働きかけを含まない関係付けの一例を報告する文となるからである。本書では、このようなある概念とその一面としての別の概念の話者による関連付けを「連想関係」と呼ぶ。そして、連想の個別的実現を「静的関係」と呼ぶことにする。更に静的関係を表す理由文を「静的理由文」と呼び、対して因果関係を表す典型的な理由文を「動的理由文」と呼ぶ。
　静的理由文の他の例をみてみよう。

(12) 静的理由文
　　　彼女は日本人だから内気だ。
　　　［偏見を込めて］

　この例文(12)と同じ文を用いて、彼女が日本人であることが原因で彼女は内気だ、という実質的領域の因果関係を表すこともできる。それは例えば、なぜ彼女が内気なのか、ということを論じる際の説明の文として可能である。だが、ここでは(12)の文は［　］内のコンテクストを踏まえて、次のような解釈で読む。(12)の文の話者は内気な日本人にたくさん接してきた経験があり、(13)の文で示されるような偏見を持っている。偏見もまた連想関係の一種である。

(13) 連想関係
　　　日本人は内気であるものだ。

　(12)の文は話者の連想関係の個別的例の報告である。その場合には、彼女が日本人であることと内気であることは共起するのであって、前者が後者を引き起こしたと考えることは適切ではなく、実質的領域のフォース・ダイナミク

スがあると判定することは難しい。
　一方で、(9) のような実質的読みの動的理由文は (14) のような因果法則の個別的実現（つまり因果関係）を報告する。

　　(14) 因果法則
　　　　大風が吹くと木が倒れる。

　本章では静的理由文の様々なヴァリエーションを分析した。一例を挙げると、(15) も (12) と同様に静的理由文だが、(12) 以上に、認識的レベルの因果関係を表しているように見える。しかし、(15) は主節述語に認識的モダリティを表す「だろう」を伴うと、同じコンテクストでは用いることができなくなることが示すように、(10) とは違って認識的読みの動的理由文の例ではない。

　　(15) 静的理由文
　　　　彼は親孝行だから偉い。

　また、本章で提案した静的理由文というカテゴリーを認めることの利点として、南 (1993) や白川 (1995) の指摘するような、「理由を表さない」理由文と、典型的な理由文との関係もより分かりやすく説明されることがある、と指摘した。
　最後に因果法則と連想関係はどのように関係しているのかを論じた。因果法則は二つの事態や状況の完全な関係付けである。一方、連想関係は不完全な関係付けであることが多い。つまり、因果法則と連想関係は関係付けの完璧さの度合いで連続していると考えられる。そして、関係付けの完璧さが低くなればなるほど、話者がそのような関係付けをしている、という話者の関係付けへの関与の度合いが大きくなる。そこでは、話者の意識の向け方（志向性）が提示される。このように、通常のフォース・ダイナミクスに基づく理由文と静的理由文、あるいは因果法則と連想関係の間には、ある特殊な「話者関与」の違いがあるといえる。次の第四章で、話者関与という観点から静的理由文を論じる。続く、第五章では静的理由文によって示される話者の志向性は、相互作用にとってどのような意味を持つのか、考える。

3-2 文法とレトリック
　第三章で扱った因果法則と連想関係の関係については、これまでは文法ではなく、主にレトリックの研究で論じられてきた。隣接関係を元にしたレトリッ

クはメトニミーであり、連想関係（カテゴリー間の包摂関係）を元にしたものはシネクドキである。それぞれ（16）と（17）に例を挙げる。

（16）メトニミー
　　　町に槌音が響く。
（17）シネクドキ
　　　白いものが降っている。

　槌音を響かせて作業をすると、その結果建築が進む。この因果関係に基づいて、（16）では槌音の響きで建築の進行を指している。一方（17）では雪には白いという性質があるので、その連想関係に基づいて白さで雪を指す。物事の隣接関係の一種である因果法則は世界に属し、連想関係は私たちの心の中にある関係付けである。本書は、カラ文の分析を通して、因果法則と連想関係の交渉をみることで、文法研究とレトリックの研究の橋渡しを目指した。

第四章：理由文と二つの話者関与度スケール

　　それでいて私は、自分が直面している困難が、日本語で「本格小説」を書く困難と通じるものであるということに気がつかざるをえなかった。大事なものが指の間からするすると滑り落ちてしまうような、何とも心もとない思い—そんな思いに書いている間中悩まされているのは、人から聞いた「小説のような話」を小説にしようとしていること、すなわち私自身の人生から離れ、「私小説」的なものから離れて書こうとしていることと無関係ではないのが見えてきたからである。私は「本格小説」を書こうとはしていなくとも、日本語で「私小説」的なものから遠く距たったものを書こうとしていることによって、日本語で「本格小説」を書く困難に直面することになったのであった。
　　　　　　　　　　　　　　　　　　　　　　（水村美苗『本格小説』）

　何かを分類するときには、分類すべき対象がどのようなものか、に着目しがちです。しかし、分類する「私」がどのようにしてその分類対象と関わるのか、ということで分けることもできます。むしろ、その方が気持ちにぴったりくることもあります。このような分類法を「ダイナミカル・カテゴリー化」と呼びましょう。第四章では、カラ文への二つの「話者関与」によって第二章と第三章で見てきたカラ文が分類されることを見ます。カラ文を語る「私」によるダイナミカル・カテゴリー化を探究します。

第二章ではカラ文の視点構造に着目し、第三章ではカラ文の表す動的関係や静的関係の、更に背後にある関係付けの完璧さの度合いによって、カラ文を分析した。この二つの分析を、第四章では、話者がカラ文で表わされる関係にどのように関わっているのか、という観点から見直した。カラ文の視点構造は、カラ文が表す関係を報告するのにどれだけ話者が関与しているか、に対応している。一方、因果法則や連想関係における関係付けの完璧さの問題は、カラ文が表す関係そのものにどれだけ話者が関与しているのかの問題である。この二つの話者関与を測るスケールでカラ文を分類した後、この二つのスケールを用いた分析手法によりカラ文とノデ文の使い分けの説明が可能であることを示した。

4-1 二つの話者関与度スケール

　Sweetser (1990) は理由の接続語に実質的読み、認識的読み、そして発話行為的読みという三つの用法があるとしたが、Maat and Degand (1991) はこれらの読みには連続性があるとし、その連続性は「話者関与度」によって捉えることができると論じた。

　まず、Maat and Degand は (18) のような非意図的な実質的読みから (19) のような意図的な実質的読みを区別する必要性を強調した。

(18) 非意図的実質的読み
　　 大風から吹いたから木が倒れた。
(19) 意図的実質的読み
　　 嫌いな子が来るから花子は祝賀会に参加しなかった。

　この区別が重要な理由として、Maat and Degand は、英語・フランス語・オランダ語などの言語において、理由の接続語が複数ある場合に、意図的実質的読みと認識的読みを表すが、非意図的実質的読みは表さない接続語があることを挙げた。そして、意図的実質的読みは、非意図的実質的読みと認識的読みの間に位置づけられるとした。このことから、Sweetser によって提案された三つの読みの間の連続性を強調し、その連続性を「話者関与度スケール (Speaker Involvement Scale)」という形で捉えた。このスケールで測ることのできる話者関与度は、(18) のような非意図的実質的読み、(19) のような意図的実質的読み、(20) のような認識的読みそして (21) のような発話行為的読み、と進むにつれ上がるとされる。

(20) 認識的読み
    明かりがついているからお隣さんはもう帰宅した。
(21) 発話行為的読み
    うるさいから静かにしなさい。

　本書は、理由の接続語の表す関係への話者の関与は一通りではない、と指摘し、Maat and Degand によって提案された話者関与度スケールを、話者関与度スケール1（SIS-1）と呼ぶことにする。そして、SIS-1 の測る話者関与とは、因果関係を見つけ出し、報告するのに話者がどれだけ関与しているか、であると解釈する。ある二つの出来事や状態を結んでいるのが因果関係かどうか、それが誰にでもはっきりしている場合とそうでない場合がある。例えば（18）における因果関係は物理法則によって支えられており、誰にでも同じように見て取ることができる。（19）のような文では事情が異なる。花子の心の中は見えないので、（19）の文を発話するにあたって話者は花子の心を推し量る。そして、花子の学校嫌いと欠席という二つのイベントを因果関係で結びつける。勿論そこには、花子の言動など話者以外にもアクセスできる手掛りはあるだろうが、物理的因果関係の場合に比べると、因果関係を抽出する際により多く話者が携わる。一方、（20）（21）のような文になると、因果関係があるということを見つけ出す手がかりは話者自身にしかない。

　SIS-1 はカラ文の表す因果関係という関係性の抽出・報告に話者がどれだけ関与するかであった。これに対し、カラ文の表す関係の成立にどれだけ話者が関わるか、を測るスケールを話者関与度スケール2（SIS-2）とする。次の例（22）を考えよう。

(22) 静的理由文
    空が青いから悲しい。

　この文によって見出され報告される関係性は、（18）から（21）の例とは異なり、因果関係とは呼び難い。因果関係の報告は情報としての価値があるが、（22）の文にはそれが欠けている。その代りに（22）の文では、（18）から（21）の文では背後に退いていた報告される関係性の成立そのものが際立つ。つまり、話者が空の青さと悲しさを関係付けているのだ、ということが提示される。この様な文は SIS-2 における話者関与度が高いとする。

　以上のようにカラ文の分析を通じて、Sweetser の分類を拡張した。二つの話者関与度を用いることで、静的理由文も説明することができる。一つ目の話者関与は因果関係を見出すのに話者の視点がどれだけ関わっているか、であり、

二つ目の関与度は理由文で表される関係付けの存在にどれだけ話者が関わっているか、である。

4-2 カラ文とノデ文の違いの分析

カラとノデの分布については多くの文献で論じられてきた。主要な研究では、以下の例文で示すような分布があることが指摘されている。(永野 [1952]、岩崎 [1995] 等に基づき Higashiizumi [2006] 他)。* は不適切な用法であることを示す。

(23) 実質的読み
　　 大風が吹いた {から・ので} 木が倒れた。
(24) 認識的読み
　　 明かりがついている {から・*ので} 彼は帰宅した。
(25) 発話行為的読み
　　 うるさい {から・*ので} 静かにしなさい。

つまり、カラは三つの読みを持ち、ノデは認識的読みと発話行為的読みでは使用が制限される。

問題は以上の広く受け入れられている分析からは (26) が説明できないことである。

(26) 母の日 {だから・なので} 花子はお母さんにカーネーションをあげた。

Miyagawa and Nakamura (1991) は (26) でノデを用いると「母の日にはカーネーションをあげるものだ」という世の中の構造を表すことになり、カラを用いると花子の行為を現象として表すことになるとした。そして、Goldsmith and Woisetschlaeger (1982) の用語を用いて、ノデ文は構造的知識を、カラ文は現象的知識を表すとした。

この分析では説明できない例が多い。まず (23) から (25) の使い分けは説明されない。また、(26) のような構造的知識を表す文で、本節末の (27) のようにノデよりカラの方が適切な場合もある。

本書では、二つの話者関与度とその相関から、(23) から (27) までの観察を全て説明できることを示した。その説明を簡単にまとめると次のようになる。主要な先行研究が示唆するように、ノデ文はカラ文と比べると SIS-1 の低い方への偏向がある。それが特に顕在化するのは、理由文の表す関係が意図的にも非意図的にも読むことができるような場合であると考えられる。この時、

ノデ文はより SIS-1 における話者関与の低い非意図的読みをとる。そして、意図的読みに比べて、非意図的読みのほうが、因果法則を見出しにくいことが多い。本書の第三章や本章で SIS-2 を導入する際に論じたように、理由文は因果法則が見出されない場合は連想関係に基づいて解釈される。つまり、SIS-2 における話者関与が高くなる。結果として（26）ではノデ文はカラ文より SIS-2 における話者関与が高い、静的理由文となっている。

　決してノデ文は常に話者関与度がカラ文より高いというわけではない。（27）のように最初から前件と後件の間にはじめから因果法則を見出しにくい文の場合にはノデ文であろうがカラ文であろうが静的理由文となる。

　　（27）静的な理由文
　　　　　海が近い｛から・ので｝ロマンチックだ。

4-3 主観性、ダイナミカル・カテゴリー化

　本章で提案した分析では、理由文が表す関係の述べ方の主観性を測るのが SIS-1 であり、関係そのものの主観性を測るのが SIS-2 である。客観的な関係を主観的に述べている例としては（20）や（21）のような認識的読み・発話行為的読みの動的理由文がある。一方で、主観的な関係を客観的に表している例としては（22）のように実質的領域の事柄を静的な関係として報告している理由文がある。

　本書の提案する二つの話者関与度を用いた分析は、主観性を二つのレベルで見たという点と、それを主観的か否かという二値的なものではなく様々な値をとりうるものとして解釈している点に特徴がある。これまでの永野（1952）以降の日本語研究の主観性による分類を精緻化したものであるとも言える。

　以上で示したようなカラ文そしてノデ文の意味の広がりを捉えることは、理由文が表す対象（例えば、フォース・ダイナミクスの種類）に注目するだけでは不十分で、理由文を用いる主体がどのように対象と関わるか（本章での話者関与）に着目して初めて可能となった。

　主体が対象と関わることによって生まれる運動に基づいたカテゴリー化は、ダイナミカル・カテゴリー化（Ikegami & Zlatev, 2008）と呼ばれる。認知言語学において重要な論点の一つとして身体性と言語の関わり（Lakoff & Johnson, 1999）が度々挙げられている。本書は話者関与によるカラ文の意味の広がりはダイナミカル・カテゴリー化の言語における例であると捉え、話者関与度という概念は身体性に基づいた言語理論の構築にあたっての重要な手がかりとなる、と論じた。

第五章：ジョイント・アテンションと文法

> エコーが本来的にエコーであるならば、エコーの話は理解不能のものとして現れることに決まっていた。エコーは、そのようにしか現れえないことを考えていた。
>
> だから、子供たちから時折向けられるこんにちはの挨拶は、エコーの敗北を意味してもいる。
>
> 会話として成り立っていなくとも、エコーが意図したものの一部は確かに、こんにちはの様相を持っていたし、子供たちがそうであると決め付けたように、ただ入り組んだだけのこんにちはの挨拶だという可能性もあった。そこで何かが通じてしまっているならば、それはエコーの敗北でしかありえなかった。
>
> （円城塔「Echo」『Self-Reference ENGINE』）

浜辺に打ち捨てられたコンピュータの「エコー」。そこから出力される信号が、いかに高度な計算に基づいていたとしても、子供たちとの相互作用においては「こんにちは」の挨拶に他なりませんでした。同じように、ある言葉の形に対して、相互作用の中ではじめて立ち現れるものがあります。第五章では、ある種のカラ文を相互作用の中に置いた時、話し手と聞き手の間に視点の共有が立ち現れるのではないか、と論じます。

前章では、様々な理由文を、理由文によって表されている関係（三人称的視点）からではなく、話者からの観点（一人称的視点）に基づいて分類する手法が有効であることを論じた。

ところで、一人称的視点から形作られた文法を想定することは、相互作用という観点を排除することにはあたらない、と指摘したい。本章では、言葉による話者の一人称的観点の提示が相互作用の中で、どのように働くのかについて、静的理由文の発話意図の問題を考えながら、論じた。

（28）のような静的理由文の発話意図は自明ではない。因果関係を報告する動的理由文は、因果関係を情報として伝えるが、静的理由文は何を情報として伝えているのだろうか。第三章で論じたように、（28）の文は因果法則に基いて因果関係を伝達する代わりに、（29）のような連想関係を抱いていることを提示していると本書では考える。では、連想関係の存在を情報として伝えているのだろうか。ならば（29）のような連想関係そのものを発話する場合と、（28）を発話する場合の違いは何だろうか。

（28）静的理由文
　　　空が青いから悲しい。
（29）連想関係
　　　私は、青空は悲しいと思っている。

　本書では静的理由文は、主に情報伝達のためではなく、志向性の方向を揃えて一致させることを目指して使われるのだ、と考える。現在の認知言語学の枠組みでは、発話の場における志向性の一致を扱う道具立てがない。そこで、発達心理学の「ジョイント・アテンション（共同注意）」（参照 Tomasello［1993］など）という概念を拡張して用い、静的理由文の発話の場における特徴を考察した。

　8から12ヶ月の幼児はコミュニケーション的身ぶりを発達させる。身ぶりコミュニケーションには二つのタイプがあるとされる。第一のタイプは「原命令」と呼ばれ、人に何かをすることを要求する身ぶりである。第二のタイプは「原叙述」と呼ばれるもので、人に特定の対象に注意を払うように求める身ぶりである（Bates, 1976）

　これまで、宇野・池上（2003, 2004）などで、Gómez、Sarria and Tamarit（1993）による「原命令」と「原叙述」の解釈を応用し、前言語的コミュニケーションと言語との関係を考えてきた。まなざしを「相手」と「対象物」に向けることで相手のまなざしを対象物に向けさせることは「ジョイント・アテンション」と呼ばれる。本書では原命令的なジョイント・アテンションは（要求などの為の）道具として用いられるので「道具的ジョイント・アテンション」、原叙述的なジョイント・アテンションはジョイント・アテンションの成立自体が目的であるので「参与的ジョイント・アテンション」と呼んでいる。（より詳しい議論は、宇野・池上［2003］。）間主観的な状態や共感を扱おうとすると多くの場合、主体の内面に直接に触れることとなり、難しい問題となる。ここで注目すべきは、参与的ジョイント・アテンションとは結果的には内面と関連するようなものではあるが、基本的には二人が同じものを見るという行為のことだ、という点である。このことで随分と相互作用の問題が扱いやすくなる。

　以後「ジョイント・アテンション」という語を拡張した意味で用いる。広義ジョイント・アテンションは成人が言語などを用いて行う行為であり、視線の向ける先を揃えるように意識を向ける先（志向性）を揃えることである。その際には話し手と聞き手以外に、第三の物が必要となるが、それは例えば言語の表す概念となる。自分・他者・物の三者の関係によって意味を生み出すというメカニズムは、本来の意味でのジョイント・アテンションと共通している。視

線を向ける先が揃うのと同様に、志向性が揃うことは、二人に「見えているもの」が同じになるということである（本多、2005）。

具体的な例で言語を用いたジョイント・アテンションを考えてみよう。(30)の文を発したならば、話し手の心は雪に向けられているが、聞き手の心は「心を雪に向けている話者」に向けられる。そのため両者の志向性は揃わない。

(30) 私は雪に感動した。

次に (30) と結果的には同じ意味を持つと考えられる (31) のような名詞一語文を発話した場合を考える（尾上、2001）。

(31) 雪。

この場合には、聞き手の意識も雪に向けられ、話し手と聞き手の両者の志向性は揃うと期待される。そこで、(31) のような感嘆を表す名詞一語文を、言語における参与的ジョイント・アテンションを引き起こす文の例と考える。

このように、話し手や聞き手を指示対象に含まず、話し手の意識にあるものだけを表すことがジョイント・アテンションを引き起こす文の特徴となる。(31) のような名詞一語文を発して結果として得られる意味が (30) の文と同じになる、と言う時、情報伝達のレベルだけを問題としている。参与的ジョイント・アテンションにおいては情報伝達ではなく、志向性を揃えるという行為の達成が重要なのである。

感嘆を表す名詞一語文と同じことが静的理由文でも議論できる。(28) の文を発話した場合には、青空と悲しみの関係付けに聞き手の心は向けられるだろう。すると、聞き手が話し手と同じ志向性を持つ可能性が高まる。一方 (29) のような発話において、聞き手は、青空と悲しみを関係づけに志向性を向けている話者に対して、志向性を向ける。従って、志向性の一致は達成できない。情報伝達の為に言語を用いるときは、話者の視点構造は、情報抽出の手掛かりとなり、聞き手によって追跡されるべきものである。第二章で見たような動的理由文の視点構造はこの例となる。一方、静的理由文は志向性の一致のために用いられることが多く、その際には視点構造は追跡されるのではなく共有されるべきものとなる。

さて、参与的ジョイント・アテンションにはヴァリエーションがあると本書は考える。前言語的な参与的ジョイント・アテンションでは、まず主体が物に心を動かされ、次にその状態をもう一人の主体と共有しようとする。言語を用いた参与的ジョイント・アテンションには、主体がもう一人の主体と何かを共

有したいということから主体が第三の物を指し示す、という場合があるのではないか、と本書は提案した。そして、そのような、対象と主体の関係ではなくて、主体と主体の関係がきっかけとなるようなジョイント・アテンションは、言語の中でも、静的理由文のように、現場性が低く、文法に支えられた言語表現によってのみ可能であると論じた。

最後に、理由文に情報伝達を機能とするもの（動的理由文）と、志向性の一致を目指すもの（静的理由文）とがあることが、平叙文一般の特徴の現れである可能性について触れた。このような可能性を追求することで、進化言語学（Steels, 2003 など）における感嘆文、命令文、平叙文といった文の種類の起源の研究を考えることができる、と論じた。

第六章：一人称的文法理論へ

一つのカラ文という形式を用いて、話者は「私」の心の中で起きていることも、「私」の外で起きていることも同じように表す。このことの背後にはどのような認知のメカニズムがあるのだろうか、と問い、本書では、カラ文の分析を行った。

まず、カラ文の実質的読みと認識的読みの違いを見た。その違いは、話者や主節主語の視点の構造（やそれと連動する接続形式）に反映されており、通常の実質的読み以外にも視点構造のヴァリエーションに対応する特殊な実質的読みがあることを指摘した。これらの特殊な実質的読みも含めて、実質的読みと認識的読みは視点構造の連続性に対応して、連続していることを指摘した。

次に、実質的読みと認識的読みの中間例にも見えるような、フォース・ダイナミクスを表さないカラ文があることを指摘した。フォース・ダイナミクスを表すカラ文から表さないカラ文へも連続性がある。それは、カラ文の背後の関係付けの客観性が背後に退き、その代わりに話者の意識が前景化するような連続性である。

以上のような二つの連続性は二つの「話者関与度」として捉え直すことができる。前者の連続性はカラ文が表す関係の報告への話者関与度として、後者の連続性はカラ文の表す関係の成立そのものへの話者関与度として測ることができる。

文の成立に発話主体がどう関わるか、という問いは極めて認知的な問題設定であるにも関わらず、認知言語学ではあまり注目されてこなかった。本書はカラ文を分析することで、「文成立への主体の関与」に着目した文法の分析手法の有効性を示した。このアプローチを「一人称的観点からの文法理論」と呼ぶことにする。

認知言語学は文法の認知的基盤を求める。本書では、カラ文の意味の広がりに関しての認知的基盤の候補として、次のようなものを提案した。視点を追跡する能力、不完全な関係付けへの偏向、ダイナミカル・カテゴリー化、ジョイント・アテンションなど。これらの項目に関しては、発達心理学において、相互作用を可能にする認知的側面としての研究がある。しかし、言語の分析と心理学における観察とは、まだまだ隔たりがある。本書では最後に、これらの認知的基盤の候補と、文法規則とをつなぐ道筋を求める工夫の一つとして、数理モデルを用いて言語や認知を考えるような研究との連携を提案した。数理モデルなどを作ることで、対象を理解しようとする立場は「構成論的アプローチ」と呼ばれる。構成論的アプローチの一つである、人工生命という研究分野では、ロボットを作ったり、コンピュータシミュレーションを行ったりすることで、生命かもしれないものが現れる様を観察する（池上, 2007 など）。そして、言語を分かりたいならば、言語かもしれないものを立ち現れさせ、観るのである。

　言語の仕組みだけではなく、どうしてこのような仕組みになっているのかという起源までも問うならば、言語のデータの分析に加えて、何らかの工夫が必要となる。一人称的観点からの文法理論の完成は十分に巧みな研究プランを作り上げることができるかどうかにかかっている。

　このようにして一人称的観点からの文法理論を目指し、本書は、日本語学でのカラ文研究への貢献に加え、認知言語学に新しい方法論を示した。また平叙文とは何かという問題を認知科学の問題として捉え直すきっかけを作り、学際的な言語研究への道が開かれることを求めた。

「内容紹介」で引用したテキストの出典
円城塔『Self-Reference ENGINE』ハヤカワ SF シリーズ・J コレクション
岡田利規「楽観的な方のケース」『新潮』2008 年 6 月号
佐藤信夫『意味の弾性』岩波書店（『レトリックの意味論』講談社学術文庫）
水村美苗『本格小説』新潮社

References

Akatsuka, Noriko. 1985. Conditionals and the epistemic scale, *Language* 61(3), 625–639.
Amihama, Shino. 1990. Conditional clauses and causal clauses [Zyookensetu to riyuusetu], *Machikaneyama Ronso* 24, 19-38.
Arita, Setsuko. 1999. Japanese conditionals and prototypical conditionality [Purototaipu kara mita nihongo no zyookenbun], *Gengokenkyu* 115, 77-108.
Austin, John. L. 1962. *How to Do Things with Words*. Oxford: Clarendon Press.
Baron-Cohen, Simon. 1995. *Mindblindness: An Essay on Autism and Theory of Mind*. Boston, MA: MIT Press.
Baron-Cohen, Simon, Helen Tager-Flusberg & Donald J. Cohen (eds.). 1993, 2000. *Understanding Others Minds: Perspectives from Autism*. Oxford: Oxford University Press.
Bates, Elizabeth. 1976. *Language and Context: the Acquisition of Pragmatics*. New York: Academic Press.
Braitenberg, Valentino. 1984. *Vehicles: Experiments in Synthetic Psychology*. Cambridge, MA: MIT Press.
Cutrer, L. Michelle. 1994. *Time and Tense in Narrative and in Everyday Language*. Ph.D. dissertation, University of California, San Diego.
Dancygier, Barbara. 1998. *Conditionals and Prediction: Time, Knowledge and Causation in Conditional Constructions*. Cambridge: Cambridge University Press.
Dancygier, Barbara. 2007. Conditional reasoning and types of alternativity, Presentation in Conditonals Workshop at University of Tokyo, Komaba.
Dancygier, Barbara & Eve Sweetser. 1996. Conditionals, distancing, and alternative spaces. In Adele E. Goldberg (ed.), *Conceptual Structure, Discourse and Language*, 83-98. Stanford: CSLI Publications.
Dancygier, Barbara & Eve Sweetser. 2000. Constructions with *if*, *since* and *because*: Causality, epistemic stance, and clause order. In Bernd Kortman & Elizabeth Traugott (eds.), *Cause-Condition-Concession-Contrast: Cognitive and Discourse Perspectives*, 111-142. Berlin: Mouton de Gruyter.
Dinsmore, John. 1991. *Partitioned Representations*. Dordrecht: Kluwer Academic Publishers.
Dowty, David. 1979. *Word Meaning and Montague Grammar*. Dordrecht: Foris.
Elman, Jeffrey L. 1998. Connectionism, artificial life, and dynamical systems. In William Bechtel & George Graham (eds.), *A Companion to Cognitive Science*, 488-505. Oxford: Basil Blackwood.
Fauconnier, Gilles. 1985, 1994. *Mental Spaces: Aspects of Meaning Construction in Natural Language*. Cambridge: MIT Press.
Fauconnier, Gilles. 1997. *Mappings in Thought and Language*. Cambridge: Cambridge University Press.
Fauconnier, Gilles & Mark Turner. 2002. *The Way We Think: Conceptual Blending and the Mind's Hidden Complexities*. New York: Basic Books.

Fillmore, Charles J. 1986. Varieties of conditional sentences, *Proceedings of the 3rd Eastern States Conference on Linguistics*, 163-182.
Fillmore, Charles J. 1990. Epistemic stance and grammatical form in English conditional sentences, *Papers from the 26th Regional Meeting of the Chicago Linguistic Society*, Vol. 1 *The Main Session*, 137-162.
Fujii, Seiko. 2000. Incipient decategorization of MONO and grammaticalization of speaker attitude in Japanese discourse. In Gisle Andersen & Torstein Fretheim (eds.), *Pragmatic Markers and Propositional Attitude*, 85-118. Amsterdam: John Benjamins.
Gärdenfors, Peter. 2008. Representing actions and functional properties in conceptual spaces. In Jordan Zlatev, Tom Ziemke, Roz Frank, & Ren Dirven (eds.), *Body, Language and Mind*, Vol. 1. Berlin: Mouton de Gruyter. 167-195.
Garrod, Simon & Martin J. Pickering. 2004. Why is conversation so easy?, *Trends in Cognitive Sciences* 8(1), 8-11.
Gergely, György & John S. Watson. 1999. Early socio-emotional development: Contingency perception and the social biofeedback model. In Philippe Rochat (ed.), *Early Social Cognition*, 101-137. Hillsdale, NJ: Erlbaum.
Gibson, James J. 1962. Observation on active touch, *Psychological Review* 69(6), 477-491.
Givón, Talmy. 1980. The binding hierarchy and the typology of complements, *Studies in Language* 4, 333-377.
Goldsmith, John, and Eric Woisetschlaeger . 1982. The logic of the English progressive, *Linguistic Inquiry* 13(1). 79-90.
Gómez, Juan Carlos, Encarnacion Sarria, & Javier Tamarit. 1993. A comparative approach to early theories of mind: ontogeny, phylogeny and pathology. In Simon Baron-Cohen, Helen Tager-Flusberg & Donald J. Cohen (eds.), *Understanding Other Minds: Perspectives from Autism*, 195-207. Oxford: Oxford University Press.
Groz, Barbara J. & Candace Sidner L. 1986. Attention, intentions, and the structure of discourse, *Computational Linguistics* 21, 203-225.
Haga, Yasushi. 1954. What is predication? [Tinzyutu to wa nanimono?], *Kokugokokubun*, 22(4).
Hasegawa, Yoko. 1996. *A Study of Japanese Clause Linkage*. Stanford: CSLI Publications.
Hauser, Marc D., Noam Chomsky, & W. Tecumseh Fitch. 2002. The faculty of language: What is it, who has it, and how did it evolve?, *Science* 298, 1569-1579.
Higashiizumi, Yuko. 2006. *From a Subordinate Clause to an Independent Clause: A History of English* because-*clause and Japanese* kara-*clause*. Tokyo: Hituzi Syobo Publishing.
Hobson, Peter. 2002. *The Cradle of Thought: Challenging the Origin of Thought*. London: Macmillan.
Honda, Akira. 2003. The syntax of joint attention [Kyoodootyuui no toogoron], *Papers in Cognitive Linguistics* 2, 199-229. Tokyo: Hituzi Syobo Publishing.
Honda, Akira. 2004. The locus of the conceptualizer in cognitive semantics [Ninti imiron ni okeru gainenka no syutai no itizuke ni tuite], *Proceedings of the Fourth annual meeting of the Japanese Cognitive Linguistics Association*, 129-139.
Honda, Akira. 2005. *An Affordance-Theoretic Approach to Cognitive Semantics [Afoodansu no nintiimiron]*. Tokyo: University of Tokyo Press.
Iizuka, Hiroyuki & Takashi Ikegami. 2004. Simulating autonomous coupling on discrimina-

tion at light frequency, *Connection Science* 16(4), 283-299.
Ikegami, Takashi. 2000. Understanding evolution of life [Seimeisinka o rikaisuru], *Parity* 15(20), 20-26.
Ikegami, Takashi. 2001. Interaction between language and cognition [Gengo to ninti no soogosayooyoosiki]. In Yukio Tsuji (ed.), *A Companion to the Cognitive Science of Language* [*Kotoba no nintikagaku ziten*], 158-175. Tokyo: Taishukan Shoten.
Ikegami, Takashi. 2004. Motion and language change [Undoo to gengo sinka], *Kagaku* 74(12), 1379-1382.
Ikegami, Takashi & Hiroyuki Iizuka. 2003. Joint attention and dynamics repertoire in coupled dynamical recognizers, *Artificial Intelligence and the Simulation of Behaviour '03 Convention*, United Kingdom, 125-130.
Ikegami, Takashi & Jordan Zlatev. 2008. From pre-representational cognition to language. In Jordan Zlatev, Tom Ziemke, Roslyn Frank, & Ren Dirven (eds.), *Body, Language and Mind*, Vol. 1. Berlin: Mouton de Gruyter. 241-283.
Iwasaki, Takashi. 1994. On tenses of *node*-clause and *kara*-clause [*Node* setu to *kara* setu no tensu ni tuite], *Kokugogaku* 179, 103-114.
Iwasaki, Takashi. 1995. *Node* and *kara* [*Node* to *kara*]. In Tatsuo Miyajima & Yoshio Nitta (eds.), *Japanese Grammar of Synonyms*, Vol.2 [Nihongo ruigigo hyoogen no bunpoo (ge)], 506-513. Tokyo: Kuroshio Shuppan.
Johnson, Mark. 1987. *The Body in the Mind: The Bodily Basis of Meaning, Imagination, and Reason*. Chicago: University of Chicago Press.
Kamp, Hans & Christian Rohrer. 1983. Tense in texts. In Rainer Bauerle, Christoph Schwarze, & Arnim von Stechow (eds.), *Meaning, Use, and Interpretation of Language*, 250-269. Berlin/New York: Walter de Gruyter.
Kawabata, Yoshiaki. 1976. Introduction to linkage and modification [Setuzoku to ren'yo ni tuite no zyosetu], *Kokugokokubun* 27(5).
Kawabata, Yoshiaki. 1985. Declinable words [Yoogen], *Iwanami Lectures in Japanese* 6 *Grammar* I [*Iwatanimi kooza nihongo* 6 *bunpoo* I], 169-217. Tokyo: Iwanami Shoten.
Kawabata, Yoshiaki. 2004. Grammar and semantics [Bunpoo to imi], *Asakura Lectures in Japanese Linguistics* 6, *Grammar* II [*Asakura nihongo kooza* 6 *bunpoo* II], 58-80. Tokyo: Asakura Syoten.
Keller, Rudi. 1995. The epistemic *weil*. In Dieter Stein & Susan Wright (eds.), *Subjectivity and Subjectivisation*, 6-30. Cambridge: Cambridge University Press.
Kindaichi, Haruhiko 1953a. The essence of undeclinable auxiliaries: the difference between subjective and objective expressions [Huhenka zyodoosi no honsitu: syukanteki hyoogen to kyakkanteki hyoogen no betu ni tuite], *Kokugokokubun* 22(2, 3).
Kindaichi, Haruhiko 1953b., The essence of undeclinable auxiliaries: In reply to Dr. Tokieda and Mr. Mizutani [Huhenka zyodoosi no honsitu: Tokieda hakase Mizutani si ryoosi ni kotaete], *Kokugokokubun* 22(9).
Kita, Sotaro. 1997. Two-dimensional semantic analysis of Japanese mimetics, *Linguistics* 35, 379-415.
Kita, Sotaro & Asli Özyürek. 2003. What does cross-linguistic variation in semantic coordination of speech and gesture reveal?: Evidence for an interface representation of spatial thinking and speaking, *Journal of Memory and Language* 48, 16-32.

Koós, Orsolya & György Gergely. 2001. The 'flickering switch' hypothesis: A contingency-based approach to the etiology of disorganized attachment in infancy. In J. Allen (ed.), *Cognitive and Interactional Foundations of Attachment, Special Issue of the Bulletin of the Menninger Clinic* 65, 397-410.

Kunihiro, Tetsuya. 1992. From *noda* to *noni* and *node* [*Noda* kara *noni/node* e]. In Hiroko Quackenbush et al. (eds.), *Japanese studies and Japanese Education* [*Nihongo kenkyu to nihongo kyooiku*]. 17-34. Nagoya: Nagoya University Press.

Kuno, Susumu, 1973. *The Structure of the Japanese Language*. Cambridge: MIT Press.

Lakoff, George. 1987. *Women, Fire and Dangerous Things: What Categories Reveal about the Mind*. Chicago: University of Chicago Press.

Lakoff, George & Mark Johnson. 1980. *Metaphors We Live By*. Chicago: University of Chicago Press.

Lakoff, George & Mark Johnson. 1999. *Philosophy in the Flesh: The Embodied Mind and Its Challenge to Western Thought*. New York: Basic Books.

Langacker, Ronald W. 1987. *Foundations of Cognitive Grammar*, Vol. I. Stanford: Stanford University Press.

Langacker, Ronald W. 1991a. *Foundations of Cognitive Grammar*, Vol. II. Stanford: Stanford University Press.

Langacker, Ronald W. 1991b. *Concept, Image, and Symbol: The Cognitive Basis of Grammar*. Berlin: Mouton de Gruyter.

Langacker, Ronald W. 2000. *Grammar and Conceptualization*. Berlin: Mouton de Gruyter.

Langacker, Ronald W. 2001. Viewing and experiential reporting in cognitive grammar. In Augusto Soares de Silva (ed.), *Linguagem e Cognição: A Perspectiva da Linguística Cognitiva*, 119-149. Braga: Associação Portuguesa de Linguística e Universidade Católica Portuguesa, Faculdade de Filosofia de Braga.

Langacker, Ronald W. 2005. On the continuous debate about discreteness, Forum lecture at 9th International Cognitive Linguistics Conference, Yonsei University, Seoul.

Loveland, Katherine & Belgin Tunali. 1993. Narrative language in autism and the theory of mind hypothesis: A wider perspective. In Simon Baron-Cohen, Helen Tager-Flusberg & Donald J. Cohen (eds.), *Understanding Other Minds: Perspectives from Autism*. 247-266. Oxford: Oxford University Press.

Lyons, John. 1977. *Semantics*, Vol. 2. Cambridge: Cambridge University Press.

Maat, Henk Pander & Liesbeth Degand. 2001. Scaling causal relations and connectives in terms of speaker involvement, *Cognitive Linguistics* 12(3), 211-245.

Maat, Henk Pander & Ted Sanders. 2001. Subjectivity in causal connectives: An empirical study of language in use, *Cognitive Linguistics* 12(3), 247-273.

Makino, Seiichi & Tsutsui Michio. 1986. *A Dictionary of Basic Japanese Grammar*. Tokyo: The Japan Times.

Marocco, Davide & Dario Floreano. 2002. Active vision and feature selection in evolutionary behavioral systems, from animals to animates, *Proceedings of the 7th International Conference on Simulation of Adaptive Behavior*, 247-255.

Maruyama, Takehiko. 1997. *Typology of Causal Connective* Kara *in Imperative Expressions* [*Meirei hyoogen ni okeru setuzokuzyosi kara no ruikei*]. MA thesis, Kobe City University of Foreign Studies.

Masuoka, Takashi. 1997. *Complex sentences* [*Fukubun*]. Tokyo: Kuroshio Shuppan.
Masuoka, Takashi & Yukinori Takubo. 1992. *Basic Japanese Grammar* [*Kiso Nihongo Bunpoo*]. Tokyo: Kuroshio Shuppan.
Matsui, Tomoko. 2003. Relevance theory [Kanrenseiriron], *Journal of the Japanese Society of Artificial Intelligence* [*Zinkootinoogakkai*] 18(5), 592-602.
Michaelis, Laura A. & Knud Lambrecht. 1996. The exclamative sentence type in English. In Adele E. Goldberg (ed.), *Conceptual Structure, Discourse and Language*, 375-389. Stanford: CSLI Publishing.
Minami, Fujio. 1974. *Structure of Current Japanese Grammar* [*Gendai nihongo no koozoo*]. Tokyo: Taishukan Shoten.
Minami, Fujio. 1993. *Outline of Current Japanese Grammar* [*Gendai nihongo bunpo no rinkaku*]. Tokyo: Taishukan Shoten.
Miyagawa, Shigeru & Mari Nakamura. 1991. The logic of *kara* and *node*. In Carol Georgopoulos & Roberta Ishihara (eds.), *Interdisciplinary Approaches to Language. Essays in Honor of S. Y. Kuroda*. 435-448. Dordrecht: Kluwer.
Mori, Yuichi. 2001. An asymmetry common to synecdoche and the part/whole metonymy [Teiyu oyobi 'zentai-bubun' 'bubun-zentai' no kan'yu ni okeru hitaisyoosei ni tuite], *Proceedings of the 1st Annual Meeting of the Japanese Cognitive Linguistics Association* 1, 12-22.
Morimoto, Gentaro & Takashi Ikegami. 2004. Evolution of plastic sensory-motor coupling and dynamic categorization, *Artificial Life IX: Proceedings of the 9th International Conference on the Simulation and Synthesis of Living Systems*, 188-193.
Mundy, Peter, Marian Sigman, & Connie Kasari. 1993. The theory of mind and joint attention deficits in autism. In Simon Baron-Cohen, Helen Tager-Flusberg & Donald J. Cohen (eds.), *Understanding Other Minds: Perspectives from Autism*, 181-203. Oxford: Oxford University Press.
Nadel, Jacqueline. 2002. Imitation and imitation recognition: Functional use in preverbal infants and nonverbal children with autism. In Andrew N. Meltzoff & Wolfgang Prinz (eds.), *The Imitative Mind: Development, Evolution, and Brain Bases*, 42-62. Cambridge: Cambridge University Press.
Nagano, Masaru. 1952. How are *kara* and *node* different from one another? [*Kara* to *node* wa doo tigau ka], *Kokugo to Kokubungaku* 29(2), 30-41.
Nagano, Masaru. 1988. Again, how are *kara* and *node* different from one another? [Saisetu *kara* to *node* to wa doo tigauka], *Nihongogaku* 12, 67–83.
Nishimura, Yoshiki. 2002. Metonymy and grammar [Kan'yu to bunpoo gensyoo]. In Yoshiki Nishimura (ed.), *Cognitive grammar*, Vol. 1 [*Nintigengogaku* I]. 285-311. Tokyo: University of Tokyo Press.
Nishimura, Yoshiki. 2005. Metonymy underlying grammar, *6th Annual Meeting of Japanese Cognitive Linguistics Conference Handbook*, 229-232.
Noda, Hisashi. 1995. Context-independent and context-dependent perspectives [Genbaizon no siten to bunmyakuizon no siten]. In Yoshio Nitta (ed.), *Studies of Complex Sentences*, Vol. 2 [*Fukubun no kenkyuu, ge*], 327-351. Tokyo: Kuroshio Shuppan.
Ohori, Toshio. 1992. *Diachrony in Clause Linkage and Related Issues*. PhD dissertation, University of California, Berkeley.

Ohori, Toshio. 2000. Constructions as linguistic knowledge [Gengo tisiki to site no koobun]. In Shigeru Sakahara (ed.), *Advances in Cognitive Linguistics* [*Nintigengogaku no hatten*], 281-315. Tokyo: Hituzi Syobo Publishing.

Ohori, Toshio. 2001. Some thoughts on a new systematization of interclausal semantic relations. Paper presented at the RRG Workshop, University of California, Santa Barbara.

Ohori, Toshio & Ryoko Uno. 2001. Grounding and knowledge structure in conditionals: towards a semantic typology of clause linkage, *English Linguistics* 17, 224-249.

Olson, Michael L. 1981. *Barai Clause Junctures: Toward a Functional Theory of Interclausal relations*. PhD dissertation, Australian National University.

Onoe, Keisuke. 1986. Exclamatory and imperative sentences [Kantanbun to kikyuu/meireibun], *Collections of Studies of Japanese Language* [*Kokugo kenkyuu ronsyuu*], 555-582. Tokyo: Meiji Shoin.

Onoe, Keisuke. 1998. The use of one-word sentences [Itigobun no yoohoo], *Collections of Studies of Japanese Language* [*Kokugo kenkyuu ronsyuu*], 888-908. Tokyo: Kyuuko Shoin.

Onoe, Keisuke. 2001. *Grammar and Meaning*, Vol.1 [*Bunpoo to imi* I]. Tokyo: Kuroshio Shuppan.

Pinker, Steven & Ray Jackendoff. 2005. The faculty of language: What's special about it?, *Cognition* 95(2), 201-236.

Premack, David & Guy Woodruff. 1978. Does the chimpanzee have a theory of mind?, *Behavioral and Brain Sciences* 4, 515-526.

Reichenbach, Hans, 1947. *Elements of Symbolic Logic*. New York: Macmillan.

Rizzolatti, Giacomo & Michael A. Arbib. 1998. Language within our grasp, *Trends in Neurosciences,* 21(5), 188-194.

Sadock, Jerrold M. & Arnold M. Zwicky. 1985. Speech act distinctions in syntax. In Timothy Shopen (ed.), *Language Typology and Syntactic Description*, Vol. 1, 155-196. Cambridge: Cambridge University Press.

Sakahara, Shigeru. 1985. *Inference in Everyday Language* [*Nitizyoo gengo no suiron*]. Tokyo: University of Tokyo Press.

Sato, Nobuo. 1986. *The Sense of Rhetoric* [*Retorikku kankaku*]. Tokyo: Koodansha.

Sato, Nobuo. 1987. *News of Rhetoric* [*Retorikku no syoosoku*]. Tokyo: Hakusuisha.

Scheier, Christian & Rolf Pfeifer. 1995. Classification as sensory-motor coordination, *Proceedings of the 3rd European Conference on Artificial life*, 657-667.

Searle, John R. 1969. *Speech Acts*. London, New York: Cambridge University Press.

Seto, Ken'ichi. 1997. Expanding metonymy [Kakudaisuru metonimii]. *Proceedings of the Kansai Linguistic Society* 17, 67-77.

Seto, Ken'ichi. 1999. Distinguishing metonymy from synecdoche. In Klaus-Uwe, Panther & Günter Radden (eds.), *Metonymy and Language and Thought*, 91-120. Amsterdam: John Benjamins.

Shirakawa, Hiroyuki. 1995. *Kara* that does not express cause [Riyuu o arawasanai *kara*]. In Nitta Yoshio (ed.), *Studies of Complex Sentences*, Vol. 1 [*Fukubunn no kenkyuu, zyoo*], 189-219. Tokyo: Kuroshio Shuppan.

Silverstein, Michael. 1976. Hierarchy of features and ergativity. In Robert Malcom Ward Dixon (ed.), *Grammatical Categories in Australian Languages*. 112-171. Canberra: Australian Institute of Aboriginal Studies, and New Jersey: Humanities Press.

Silverstein, Michael. 1993. Of nominatives and datives: Universal grammar from the bottom up. In Robert D. Van Valin, Jr. (ed.), *Advances in Role and Reference Grammar*, 465-498. Amsterdam: John Benjamins.
Slobin, Dan I. 2004. The many ways to search for a frog: Linguistic typology and the expression of motion events. In Sven Strömqvist & Ludo Verhoeven (eds.), *Relating Events in Narrative:* Vol. 2. *Typological and Contextual Perspectives*, 219-257. Mahwah, NJ: Lawrence Erlbaum Associates.
Steels, Luc. 2003. Evolving grounded communication for robots, *Trends in Cognitive Science* 7(7), 308-312.
Steels, Luc. 2005. The recruitment theory of language origins, Draft for the Morris Symposium on Language Evolution, Stony Brook.
Sweetser, Eve. 1990. *From Etymology to Pragmatics: Metaphorical and Cultural Aspects of Semantic Structure*. Cambridge: Cambridge University Press.
Sweetser, Eve. 1996. Mental spaces and the grammar of constructions. In Gilles Fauconnier & Eve Sweetser (eds.), *Spaces, Worlds, and Grammar*, 318-333. Chicago: University of Chicago Press.
Sweetser, Eve. 2007. Conditionality, embedding, and viewpoint, Presentation at Conditonals Workshop at University of Tokyo, Komaba.
Sweetser, Eve & Barbara Dancygier. 2005. *Mental Spaces in Grammar: Conditional Constructions*. Cambridge: Cambridge University Press.
Sweetser, Eve & Lilian Ferrari. 2007. Subjectivity and upwards projection in mental space structure, *Handbook of 10th International Cognitive Linguistics Conference*, 81.
Tager-Flusberg, Helen. 2000. Language and understanding minds: connections in autism. In Simon Baron-Cohen, Helen Tager-Flusberg, & Donald J. Cohen (eds.), *Understanding Other Minds: Perspectives from Developmental Cognitive Neuroscience* (2nd ed.), 124-149. Oxford: Oxford University Press.
Takahashi, Taro. 1993, 2005. *Japanese Grammar [Nihongo no bunpoo]*. Tokyo: Hituzi Syobo Publishing.
Takubo, Yukinori. 1987. Syntactic structure and contextual information [Toogokoozoo to bunmyakuzyoohoo], *Nihongogaku* 6(5), 37-48.
Takubo, Yukinori. 1992. Theory of mental spaces [Mentarusupeesu riron], *Gengo* 21(12), 54-56.
Talmy, Leonard. 1988. Force dynamics in language and cognition, *Cognitive Science* 2, 49-100.
Talmy, Leonard. 2000. *Toward a Cognitive Semantics*, Vol. 2. Cambridge: MIT Press.
Tani, Jun & Stefano Nolfi. 1998. Learning to perceive the world as articulated, *Proceedings of the 5th International Conference on Simulation of Adative Behavior*, 270-279.
Teramura, Hideo. 1984. *Syntax and Semantics of Japanese,* Vol.2 *[Nihongo no sintakusu to imi* II]. Tokyo: Kuroshio Shuppan.
Tio, Sanbun. 1988. *Kara* and *node [Kara* to *node], Nihongogaku* 7, 63-77.
Tokieda, Motoki. 1950. Expressions of predication in predicates [Yoogen ni okeru tinzyutu no hyoogen], *Grammar of Spoken Japanese [Nihongo bunnpoo koogo hen]*. Tokyo: Iwanami Shoten.
Tomasello, Michael. 1999. *The Cultural Origins of Human Cognition.* Cambridge: Harvard University Press.

Tomasello, Michael. 2003. *Constructing a Language: A Usage-Based Theory of Language Acquisition.* Cambridge: Harvard University Press.

Trevarthen, Colwyn. 1993. The self born in intersubjectivity: The psychology of an infant communicating. In Ulric Neisser (ed.), *The Perceived Self*, 121-172. Cambridge: Cambridge University Press.

Tsuda, Ichiro & Takashi Ikegami. 2002. A book review on *Endophysics*, *Discrete Dynamics in Nature and Society* 7, 213-214.

Uno, Ryoko. 2001. Introducing speaker's construal in semantic relations hierarchy: A case of Japanese causal clauses, *3rd Role and Reference Grammar International Conference Handbook*, 56.

Uno, Ryoko. 2006 Cognitive analysis of complex sentences with causal connectives [Riyuu setu o fukumu fukubun no nintiteki bunseki], *Gengo Joho Kagaku* 4, 35-49. Tokyo: Department of Language and Information Sciences, University of Tokyo

Uno, Ryoko & Takashi Ikegami. 2003. Joint attention/prediction and language [Zyointo atensyon / yosoku to gengo]. *Papers in Cognitive Linguistics* 2, 231-274. Tokyo: Hituzi Syobo Publishing.

Uno, Ryoko & Takashi Ikegami. 2005. Causal connectives and active perception [Itininsyooteki setumei ni yoru riyuubun no bunseki], *Proceedings of the 4th Annual Meeting of the Japanese Cognitive Linguistics Association*, 73-83.

Uno, Ryoko, Davide Marocco, Stefano Nolfi & Takashi Ikegami. 2008. Emergence of sentence types in simulated adaptive agents, *The Evolution of Language: Proceedings of the 7th International Conference*, 323-330.

Van Valin, Robert D., Jr. 1993. A synopsis of role and reference grammar. In Robert D. Van Valin, Jr. (ed.), *Advances in Role and Reference Grammar*, 1-164. Amsterdam: John Benjamins.

Van Valin, Robert D., Jr. 2001. The acquisition of complex sentences: A case study in the role of theory in the study of language development, In John Boyle, Jung-Hyuck Lee, & Arika Okrent (eds.), *Chicago Linguistic Society* 36(2), 511-531.

Van Valin, Robert D., Jr. 2005. *Exploring the Syntax-Semantics Interface.* Cambridge: Cambridge University Press.

Van Valin, Robert D., Jr. & Randy Lapolla. 1997. *Syntax.* Cambridge: Cambridge University Press.

Van Valin, Robert D., Jr. & David P. Wilkins. 1993. Predicting syntactic structure from semantic representations. In Robert D. Van Valin, Jr. (ed.), *Advances in Role and Reference Grammar*, 499-534. Amsterdam: John Benjamins.

Varela, Francisco. 1992. Autopoiesis and a biology of intentionality. In Barry McMullin & Noel Murphy (eds.), *Autopoiesis and Perception: A Workshop with ESPRIT BRA 3352*, Addendum to the print proceedings distributed during the workshop at Dublin City University.

Verhargen, Arie. 2000. The girl who promised to become something: An exploration into diachronic subjectification in Dutch. In Thomas F. Shannon & Johan P. Snapper (eds.), *The Berkeley Conference on Dutch Linguistics 1997: The Dutch Language at the Millennium*, 197-208. Lanham, MD: University Press of America.

Verhargen, Arie. 2005. *Constructions of Intersubjectivity. Discourse, Syntax, and Cognition.* Ox-

ford: Oxford University Press.
Watanabe, Minoru. 1953. Predication and description [Tinnzyutu to zyozyutu], *Kokugogaku* 13, 14.
Yamada, Yoshio. 1908. *Theory of Japanese Grammar [Nihon bunpoo ron]*. Tokyo: Hobunkan.
Yamada, Yoshio. 1936. *Introduction to Japanese Grammar [Nihon bunpoogaku gairon]*. Tokyo: Hobunkan.
Yamashita, Hideo. 1986. *Japanese Language and Mind [Nihon no kotoba to kokoro]*. Tokyo: Kodansha.
Zlatev, Jordan. 2002.Mimesis: The 'missing link' between signals and symbols in phylogeny and ontology?. In Anneli Pajunen (ed.), *Mimesis, Sign and Language Evolution, Publications in General Linguistics* 3, 93-122. Finland: University of Turku.

Index

a
A (E-M) 27
artificial life 107
association 67, 75, 83, 92, 104, 113

c
carnation sentence 82
causal law 45, 46, 104
causation 46, 49
clausal order 40, 109
cognitive domain 69
cognitive linguistics 9, 12, 15, 105, 108
complex sentence 106
conditional 12, 13, 111
connective 1, 8
connotative relation 46, 49, 62, 67, 113
content reading 10, 31, 38, 42, 69, 78, 103
contingency 75
coordination 23, 40, 42
cosubordination 23, 40
CSJ 47

d
D (E-M) 27
daroo 36, 47, 54
declarative 98, 99, 100
deictic center 21
developmental psychology 107
doosite 60
dynamical categorization 90, 108
dynamic causal 93, 104
dynamic *kara* sentence 51

e
E-D 25
E-M 25
epistemic modality 24, 34, 37
epistemic reading 10, 31, 38, 42, 70, 78, 103
epistemic stance 12, 110
evolutionary linguistics 100, 108
exclamation 95
exclamative 98, 100

f
first-person point of view 2, 105, 106
force dynamics 12, 46, 48
form/meaning linking 12, 42
functional linguistics 12, 15

g
ground-dependent joint attention 97, 99, 114
ground-independent joint attention 98, 99

i
imperfect contingency 64, 76, 92, 107
information 93, 100
instrumental JA 94

intentionality 64, 75, 91, 93, 100, 104
Interclausal Relations Hierarchy 23
interface 105
IRH 24, 42

j
Japanese linguistics 3, 88
joint attention 91, 93, 94, 97
juncture 22

l
less volitional 84
logical connectives 10

m
mental space 13, 37, 38, 99, 109, 110
metaphor 10
metonymy 45, 46
Minami's model 8
mono 62
mono-da-kara 111
mono-da 62

n
nara 12
nexus 22, 42
node 3, 7, 79, 80, 82
non-past tense 25
non-volitional 14, 69, 70, 78,

o
one-word sentence 95, 96
operators 22
ordinary content 20, 78

p

participatory JA 94, 96, 100, 107
past tense 24, 37
perfect contingency 64
perspective 19, 37, 73, 92, 107, 110, 111
perspective structure 19, 42
phenomenal knowledge 82
prejudice 83
private association 83
pronoun 41
propositional attitude. 63
protagonist 20, 72
proto-declarative 94
proto-imperative 93

r

redundant 93, 114
request 95
Role and Reference Grammar 21
RRG 21, 42

s

SAC 33, 38, 73
SAC-1 33, 38, 73, 78
SAC-2 33, 38, 73, 78
SE 25
sentence type 98
si 61
simple sentence 106
SIS 67, 68
SIS-1 74, 77, 80, 89
SIS-2 74, 78, 83, 89, 91
speaker involvement scale 67, 70, 72, 74, 104
speech act reading 10, 11, 58, 61, 70
static causal 79, 93, 96, 104
static *kara* sentence 51
static predicate 56
static relation 49, 92, 112
structural knowledge 82
subjectivity 2, 7, 88, 90
subordination 23, 40, 42
synecdoche 45, 46

t

tense 24, 37
tense-suspended *kara* clause 32
theory of mind 98, 107, 113
third-person point of view 2, 105, 106
tradition 83

v

viewpoint 37
volitional 14, 70, 78, 84
V-point 37

y

yooda 34

【著者紹介】

宇野 良子（うのりょうこ）

1973年東京都武蔵野市生まれ。国際基督教大学教養学部語学科を卒業。東京大学大学院総合文化研究科言語情報科学専攻修士課程、博士課程を修了。博士（学術）。現在、東京大学特任研究員。慶応義塾大学他にて非常勤講師。

〈主な著書〉「接続助詞『から』と『ので』を含む複文の認知的分析―発話の場のダイナミズムと文法―」森雄一・西村義樹・山田進・米山三明（編）『ことばのダイナミズム』くろしお出版、51-67.(2008)。「ジョイント・アテンション／予測と言語―志向性を揃えるメカニズム―」山梨正明（編）『認知言語学論考 No.2』ひつじ書房、231-274.(2003) 池上高志氏との共著。

Hituzi Linguistics in English No.12

Detecting and Sharing Perspectives Using Causals in Japanese

発行	2009年2月14日 初版1刷
定価	12000円＋税
著者	© 宇野良子
発行者	松本 功
装丁	向井裕一（glyph）
印刷所	三美印刷株式会社
製本所	田中製本印刷株式会社
発行所	株式会社 ひつじ書房

〒112-0011 東京都文京区千石2-1-2 大和ビル2F
Tel.03-5319-4916 Fax 03-5319-4917
郵便振替 00120-8-142852
toiawase@hituzi.co.jp http://www.hituzi.co.jp/

ISBN978-4-89476-405-7　C3080

造本には充分注意しておりますが、落丁・乱丁などがございましたら、小社かお買上げ書店にておとりかえいたします。ご意見、ご感想など、小社までお寄せ下されば幸いです。

刊行案内

Hituzi Linguistics in English No.10
The Development of the Nominal Plural Forms in Early Middle English
堀田隆一 著
978-4-89476-403-3　定価 13000 円 + 税

Hituzi Linguistics in English No.11
Chunking and Instruction
The Place of Sounds, Lexis, and Grammar in English Language Teaching
中森誉之 著
978-4-89476-404-0　定価 8800 円 + 税

Hituzi Linguistics in English No.12
Detecting and Sharing Perspectives Using Causals in Japanese
宇野良子 著
978-4-89476-405-7　定価 12000 円 + 税

Hituzi Linguistics in English No.13
Discourse Representation of Temporal Relations in the So-Called Head-Internal Relatives
石川邦芳 著
978-4-89476-406-4　定価 9400 円 + 税

Hituzi Linguistics in English No.14
Features and Roles of Filled Pauses in Speech Communication
A corpus-based study of spontaneous speech
渡辺美知子 著
978-4-89476-407-1　定価 11000 円 + 税

刊行案内

講座社会言語科学　全6巻
各巻 A5判上製カバー装　定価3200円＋税

講座社会言語科学 第1巻　異文化とコミュニケーション
井出祥子・平賀正子 編

講座社会言語科学 第2巻　メディア
橋元良明 編

講座社会言語科学 第3巻　関係とコミュニケーション
大坊郁夫・永瀬治郎 編

講座社会言語科学 第4巻　教育・学習
西原鈴子・西郡仁朗 編

講座社会言語科学 第5巻　社会・行動システム
片桐恭弘・片岡邦好 編

講座社会言語科学 第6巻　方法
伝康晴・田中ゆかり 編

シリーズ文と発話　全3巻　串田秀也・定延利之・伝康晴 編
各巻 A5判上製カバー装　定価3200円＋税

第1巻　活動としての文と発話
第2巻　「単位」としての文と発話
第3巻　時間の中の文と発話

刊行案内

国際交流基金日本語教授法シリーズ　全14巻
各巻B5判並製（* は2009年2月現在未刊）

- 第1巻　日本語教師の役割／コースデザイン　定価580円＋税
- 第2巻　音声を教える　定価1500円＋税
- *第3巻　文字・語彙を教える
- *第4巻　文法を教える
- 第5巻　聞くことを教える　定価1000円＋税
- 第6巻　話すことを教える　定価800円＋税
- 第7巻　読むことを教える　定価700円＋税
- *第8巻　書くことを教える
- 第9巻　初級を教える　定価700円＋税
- *第10巻　中・上級を教える
- *第11巻　日本事情・日本文化を教える
- *第12巻　学習を評価する
- *第13巻　教え方を改善する
- 第14巻　教材開発　定価800円＋税